WALKING IN
COUNTY DURHAM

WALKING IN
COUNTY DURHAM

40 WALKING ROUTES EXPLORING PENNINE MOORS, RIVER VALLEYS AND COASTAL PATHS

by Paddy Dillon

JUNIPER HOUSE, MURLEY MOSS,
OXENHOLME ROAD, KENDAL, CUMBRIA LA9 7RL
www.cicerone.co.uk

© Paddy Dillon 2022
Fifth edition 2022
ISBN: 978 1 78631 137 5
Fourth edition 2019
Third edition 2015
Second edition 2008
First edition 1996

Printed in Singapore by KHL Printing using responsibly sourced paper

A catalogue record for this book is available from the British Library.
All photographs are by the author.

© Crown copyright 2022. OS PU100012932.

Updates to this Guide

While every effort is made by our authors to ensure the accuracy of guidebooks as they go to print, changes can occur during the lifetime of an edition. Any updates that we know of for this guide will be on the Cicerone website (www.cicerone.co.uk/1137/updates), so please check before planning your trip. We also advise that you check information about such things as transport, accommodation and shops locally. Even rights of way can be altered over time. We are always grateful for information about any discrepancies between a guidebook and the facts on the ground, sent by email to updates@cicerone.co.uk or by post to Cicerone, Juniper House, Murley Moss, Oxenholme Road, Kendal LA9 7RL.

Register your book: To sign up to receive free updates, special offers and GPX files where available, register your book at www.cicerone.co.uk.

Front cover: Grassholme Reservoir (Walk 25)

CONTENTS

Map key 6

INTRODUCTION 11
Getting to County Durham 12
Getting around County Durham 13
Geology 15
Flowers and animals 18
Scenery 20
Mining 21
Railways 23
Access to the countryside 24
Maps 26
What's the walking like? 26
Walking and the weather 26
Tourist information and visitor centres 28
Emergencies 29
How to use this guidebook 30

ROUTES
1   Durham City and the River Wear 32
2   Bearpark, Broompark and Brandon 36
3   Dipton and Hamsterley Mill 41
4   Beamish and Causey 44
5   Ouston and Urpeth 49
6   Lumley Castle and Great Lumley 51
7   Durham Coast Path 55
8   Castle Eden Dene 62
9   Wingate and Station Town 67
10 Cassop and Quarrington 70
11 Sedgefield and Hardwick Hall 74
12 Middleton One Row and Girsby 78
13 Low and High Coniscliffe 81
14 Gainford and Piercebridge 84
15 Cockfield Fell and Butterknowle 88
16 Woodland and Copley 92
17 Staindrop and Cleatlam 95
18 Greta Bridge and Brignall Banks 99

19 Tan Hill and Sleightholme Moor 102
20 Bowes and Bowes Moor 105
21 Barnard Castle and the Tees 110
22 Cotherstone and Romaldkirk 114
23 Tees Railway Walk 118
24 Middleton and Monk's Moor 122
25 Middleton and Grassholme 128
26 Low Force and High Force 132
27 Holwick and Hagworm Hill 137
28 Mickle Fell via the Boundary Route 142
29 Cronkley Fell 145
30 Cow Green and Widdybank Fell 148
31 Cow Green and Herdship Fell 153
32 Bishop Auckland and Binchester 156
33 Circuit of Crook 160
34 Wolsingham and Frosterley 164
35 Wolsingham and Tunstall Reservoir 169
36 Stanhope and Stanhope Dene 173
37 Westgate, Middlehope and Rookhope 178
38 Chapelfell Top and Noon Hill 182
39 Cowshill, Killhope and Allenheads 186
40 Edmundbyers and Edmundbyers Common 191

Appendix A   Route summary table 194
Appendix B   Useful contacts 196

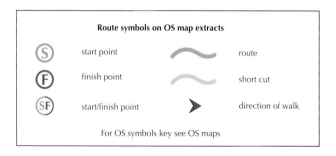

Route symbols on OS map extracts

Ⓢ   start point

Ⓕ   finish point

Ⓢ︎Ⓕ   start/finish point

〜   route

〜   short cut

❯   direction of walk

For OS symbols key see OS maps

A blaze of gorse bushes on the cliff coast between
Hawthorn Dene and Easington Colliery (Walk 7)

A track rises from Stanhope Dene
to Park Plantation (Walk 36)

Looking across the River Wear to Durham Cathedral (Walk 1)

INTRODUCTION

County Durham stretches from the high Pennines in the west to a low cliff-coast in the east. Its richly wooded, ancient landscape covered a treasure trove of coal and lead. Wave after wave of invaders fought each other, conquered each other and settled beside each other to breed a race of hardy people who will always have the strength to face change – for County Durham is essentially a land of change.

Durham city is dominated by symbols of a powerful trinity. The cathedral is a symbol of religious power; the castle a symbol of civic power; the university a symbol of the power of thought and learning. This trinity of powers and disciplines was personified in a succession of 'prince-bishops', who dominated and controlled the region throughout centuries of change. The religio-political scene was summed up in the words of Sir Walter Scott:

'Grey towers of Durham!
Yet well I love thy mixed
and massive piles
Half church of God, half castle
'gainst the Scot'.

Those who walk through County Durham can best observe the signs of change. Here you will find a Roman fort, and over there a Saxon church or a Norman castle. Here is a coalmine, there is a lead mine, and over there is an old stone quarry. You can find remnants of ancient woodland, marvel at communities of arctic/alpine plants, or observe the slow and steady reclamation of a former industrial site by the forces of nature. Ancient market towns, old pit villages and new industrial sites all share the same countryside.

As industry changes, its remains are consigned to museums and visitor centres, so a generation is growing up who will never experience the depths of a coalmine, and are breathing cleaner air. As former industrial sites are redeveloped for recreational uses, there are more opportunities to explore new areas of countryside, where interpretative facilities are first class.

County Durham is changing fast. Historically, it was a land hemmed in between two mighty rivers – the Tyne to the north and the Tees to the south. It lost portions of its original territory in the local government reorganisation of 1974, although it gained a generous slice of Yorkshire in the process. In 1997 the Borough of Darlington 'seceded' from County Durham, so the county boundary keeps shifting. The power of the prince-bishops has waned, and more and more people are turning to the countryside to find a renewal of spirit. There are broad and bleak moorlands to explore, wide-ranging views to enjoy, powerful

waterfalls to admire, woodlands and fields to wander through, heritage sites to visit, with plenty of interest and enjoyment on the way.

The network of rights of way is constantly being overhauled by an active Countryside Group at County Hall, with the aim of ensuring that paths are walkable and clearly marked. New routes are being developed, most notably a splendid, signposted network of traffic-free cycleways along old railway track-beds, linking with cycleways along quiet country roads. The Countryside and Rights of Way Act 2000 ensures that a high degree of access is available to walkers on the bleak and remote moorlands of the North Pennines. Tourism is an important new industry for County Durham.

This guidebook contains detailed descriptions of 40 one-day walks spread all over County Durham, to illustrate the region's history, heritage, countryside and natural wonders. The terrain covered ranges from field paths to open moorlands, from the North Sea to the high Pennines. You will be able to discover the region's geology, natural history and heritage by following informative trails, or taking in specific sites of interest along the way. A network of tourist information centres can help you discover the best places to stay, how to get around and what to see. Welcome to 'Walking in County Durham – the Land of the Prince-Bishops'.

GETTING TO COUNTY DURHAM

By air

The two airports most convenient for getting to County Durham are Newcastle (www.newcastleairport. com) and Teesside International Airport (www.teessideinternational. com). There are more flights to and from the former than the latter.

By sea

Ferries reach Newcastle from Amsterdam, bringing the region within reach the Low Countries. Check ferries with DFDS Seaways (www.dfds.com).

By rail

County Durham prides itself on being the 'cradle of the railways', and so arriving by rail ties in well with the heritage of the region. LNER provides direct rail services to Durham from London Kings Cross and also from Edinburgh (www.lner.co.uk). CrossCountry also runs direct services to Durham from points as far afield as Birmingham, Edinburgh and Glasgow (www.crosscountrytrains. co.uk).

By bus

National Express coaches has direct services from London Victoria coach station to Durham, and also from Newcastle, Doncaster and Portsmouth (www.nationalexpress.com). Arriva (www.arrivabus.co.uk) and Go North East (www.gonortheast.co.uk) buses cover the region and Durham is a hub in their networks.

GETTING AROUND COUNTY DURHAM

Public transport around County Durham is generally excellent, with most places enjoying regular daily bus services.

If relying on buses, be sure to check the relevant timetables in

A rough-surfaced road crosses Bowes Moor and links with the course of the Pennine Way (Walk 19)

Castle Eden Dene is managed as a national nature reserve and contains ancient woodland (Walk 8)

advance, and ensure that the level of service allows time to complete a walk. All the bus operators have websites showing timetables, and Google Maps 'directions' can be used to check timetable details.

Few places are accessible by rail, but a handful of important destinations are served. Public transport around County Durham is excellent in most places and quite good in others. In fact, it is good enough to be relied upon by walkers who wish to travel without a car. This guidebook was researched using public transport from one end of County Durham to the other, without any problems. However, some services have been drastically reduced recently.

By rail

Considering County Durham's railway heritage, and the fact that the region was comprehensively criss-crossed by railways in the 19th century, the 21st century network is a mere skeleton service. The mainline railway links Newcastle, Durham and Darlington. The coastal railway links the mainline railway with Stockton-on-Tees, Hartlepool, Seaham and Sunderland and one day the branch line from Darlington to Bishop Auckland may carry passengers into Weardale. For now, most local rail services in County Durham are provided by Northern (www. northernrailway.co.uk). The heritage Weardale Railway (www.weardale-railway.org.uk) operates only between Wolsingham, Frosterley and

Stanhope, but has plans to extend its services in the future.

By bus

Arriva traces its origins to an enterprise run by the Cowie family of Sunderland in 1938, and now provides the bulk of bus services in County Durham, www.arrivabus.co.uk. Go-North East buses generally operates in the northern parts of County Durham, linking with Newcastle, www.gonortheast.co.uk. There are half-a-dozen minor bus operators, of which the most important is Weardale Travel, which operates across the whole of Weardale, www.weardale-travel.co.uk.

Some bus operators sell 'explorer' tickets, offering exceptional value when a long journey or a change of bus is involved. Explorer North East tickets allow buses from several operators to be used. See www.networkonetickets.co.uk for full details.

Bus services around County Durham can be checked on the County Council website at www.durham.gov.uk/busmap.

Traveline

Timetable information can be checked for any form of public transport in County Durham and beyond by contacting Traveline, tel 0871 2002233, www.traveline.info.

GEOLOGY

The geology of County Durham is complex, but its salient points can be

A gentle stretch of the River Tees between Low Force and High Force (Walk 26)

presented in a simplified manner. An understanding of the geology of the region helps to interpret the development of its landforms, scenery and industries. Starting at the very bottom, the ancient bedrock does not outcrop anywhere, but the Weardale Granite was ultimately 'proved' and brought to the surface from a bore-hole drilled at Rookhope in 1961. Until that time, its existence was inferred from broken specimens found in ancient conglomerates.

The whole of this region was once covered by a warm, shallow tropical sea. Countless billions of shelled, soft-bodied creatures lived and died in this sea. Coral reefs grew, and even microscopic organisms sometimes had some sort of hard external or internal structure. Over the aeons, these creatures left their hard shells in heaps on the seabed, and these deposits became the massive grey limestone seen in the Durham Dales today.

However, even while the limestone was being laid down, distant mountain ranges were being worn away by storms, and vast rivers brought mud, sand and gravel down into the sea. These murky deposits reduced the light in the water, and caused delicate coral reefs and other creatures to die. As more mud and sand was washed into the sea, a vast delta system spread across the region. At times, shoals of sand and gravel stood above the water-line, and these became colonised by strange, fern-like trees.

The level of water in the rivers and sea was in a state of fluctuation, and sometimes the forested delta would be completely flooded, so that plants would be buried under more sand and gravel. This compressed plant material within the beds of sand and mud became thin bands of coal, known as the coal measures. The alternating series of sandstones and mudstones, with occasional seams of coal, can be seen all the way across the county, and the various hard and soft layers in this sedimentary series can often be detected today, where the hill slopes have a vaguely stepped appearance.

In a later era, another warm, shallow sea covered the region, but this was landlocked, and gradually shrinking by evaporation. Salts which the sea held in solution became so concentrated that they ultimately crystallised out of the water in a fine suspension and were deposited on the seabed. The first compounds to be precipitated out of solution were calcium carbonate and magnesium carbonate. These formed the dolomitic, or magnesian limestone which is now found in eastern Durham. These soft, banded rocks break down into a mineral-rich soil favouring certain types of plants. A vague ridge of these

rocks runs along the eastern side of the county, ending in a low cliff-line abutting the North Sea.

Other geological processes in this region were more violent, resulting in the fracturing and tilting of the ordered sedimentary deposits. The whole series is tilted so that the rocks exposed in the Pennines are older than those exposed by the sea. The hard bed of rock known as the Whin Sill arrived as a sheet of molten material, squeezed, under intense heat and pressure, in between the Pennine limestone beds. It baked the surrounding limestone, altering its nature. Wherever the Whin Sill appears, it proves to be more resistant to weathering than the surrounding limestone, so it forms cliffs on the hillsides and dramatic waterfalls where it appears in riverbeds. In Teesdale it has been

Fossiliferous Frosterley marble is one of the most striking rocks quarried in County Durham

Outcrops of 'sugar limestone' should be inspected for wild flowers, on the way past Cow Green Reservoir (Walk 30)

quarried in many locations, being prized as a durable road-stone.

Deep-seated heat and pressure also brought streams of super-heated, mineral-rich liquids and vapours into cracks and joints in the rocks. These condensed to form veins of mixed minerals, which included lead, silver and copper. Associated minerals included barytes, quartz, fluorspar, calcite, and a host of other compounds. Generally, lead mines and most stone quarries are found in the Pennines; old coalmines occur in the central parts of County Durham. In more recent decades, miners dug down through the soft magnesian limestone to reach previously untapped coal a long way below, extending their workings far beneath the bed of the North Sea.

A geological study of County Durham could be as difficult and as detailed as you wish, and the above describes just the bare bones of the landscape. Many low-lying parts of the region are covered by thick deposits of glacial drift, and have tended to develop a more agricultural outlook, especially in the southern parts of the county.

FLOWERS AND ANIMALS

Left to its own devices, without human interference and intensive sheep grazing, County Durham would eventually revert to deciduous forest. This would undoubtedly be dense on low-lying land and in the dales, with sparser cover on higher ground – few areas would be left completely without forest cover. It is thought that only tiny areas of the original, native 'wildwoods' remain. The woods of Castle Eden Dene (Walk 8) in the east of the county, and possibly the juniper thickets of Upper Teesdale (Walk 26) in the west may be all that remain.

In 1635 some 1400 stout trees were felled near Willington and taken to Woolwich to construct the navy's first three-decker ship, *Sovereign of the Seas.* Other woods were developed as coppices to ensure a constant supply of fuel for iron smelting. Almost all of the trees seen today around County Durham are secondary plantings, no matter how well established they may seem, or how natural they may look in their settings.

Many visitors are delighted to visit Upper Teesdale in spring and early summer, where the peculiar 'Teesdale Assemblage' of plant communities is seen to best effect. Remnant arctic/alpine plants thrive on bleak moorlands, such as cloudberries on the boggiest parts. Drier areas, particularly where the soil is generated by crumbly 'sugar limestone', on Cronkley Fell (Walk 29) and Widdybank Fell (Walk 30), feature an abundance of artic/alpines, including the delightful spring gentian and mountain pansy. Curious woodland plants, deprived of their original shade, now grow in the shade provided by boulders.

Other plants thrive in hay meadows, because haymaking traditionally starts late at Upper Teesdale and Weardale, allowing seeds to mature and drop before mowing. A trip to the Bowlees visitor centre (tel 01833 622145) is a fine way to get to grips with the nature and flora of the region before setting off walking and exploring (Walk 26).

Remember that the extensive grass and heather moors of the Pennines exist only because of human intervention. The grassy moors were developed as rough pasture, and the heather moors to provide food and shelter for grouse, to maintain a grouse-shooting industry. Without the intervention of man, there would be a greater range of species on the moors, including trees, and in areas where the blanket bog is eroding, the roots of ancient pines and birch trees are exposed thousands of years after their death.

Mountain pansies are abundant around the head of Teesdale and Weardale

Cloudberry, an arctic/alpine remnant plant that prefers boggy moors, grows abundantly on Mickle Fell

Sudden changes of rock type influence the plants that will be found – soil can range from very acid to very alkaline throughout County Durham, often because of the underlying rock. In the Pennines vegetation can differ when the underlying rock changes from sandstone to limestone. The 'sugar limestone' of Upper Teesdale supports different plant communities from those found in the surrounding boggy moors, and the magnesian limestone of eastern Durham supports yet other types of grasses and species of flower.

In more intensive agricultural areas, farmers decide what will or will not grow on a seasonal basis. To observe wild plants in these areas, look along the hedgerows that bound the fields, scout around marginal land, or study land that is left uncultivated. In early summer, brilliant blazes of oilseed rape put even the cheery all-year-round gorse bloom into the shade. (One hopes that rubbery stalks will not be tangled across the paths, and that the plants encountered enhance, rather than hinder your walk!)

Most of the animal life to be seen in County Durham will be farm stock, although deer are present in some wooded areas and they might be observed grazing along the margins of woods and forests at dawn and dusk. Birdlife, on the other hand, can be rich and varied, due to the range of habitats across the county.

The North Pennines are notable for red grouse, and the moorlands are often managed to favour large populations of these birds, even if it means controlling other species in the process. Rare black grouse can occasionally be spotted, especially during the mating season, when they perform elaborate displays on particular parts of the moors. The place name Cocklake is derived from 'cock lek', and refers to the mating displays of black grouse. While colonies of gulls and waders can be seen on the Durham coast, some species will also travel to the Pennines, and it is not unusual to find raucous gulleries high on the moors.

One notable local species is the northern brown argus butterfly, whose caterpillars favour feeding on the rock-rose, which itself thrives on the kind of soils found on magnesian limestone, which is common in the eastern part of the county, and around Castle Eden Dene (Walk 8).

SCENERY

The scenery of County Durham is largely dependent upon the underlying geology, but also depends on land use. There are distinct scenic regions within the county, with marked differences between the high ground in the west and the low-lying ground in the east. The Pennines dominate the western half of County Durham, and are largely extensive moorlands with broad, bleak, rounded summits. They may be grassy or heathery, with very few trees and forests.

The two great rivers in this part of the Pennines are the Tees and

Teesdale and the River Tees are among the most scenic places in County Durham (Walk 26)

the Wear, flanked by the Derwent and the Greta. The valley floors of Teesdale and Weardale are lush and green, with sheep pastures and meadows crisscrossed by stone walls and hedgerows, dotted with solid farmsteads and small woodlands.

As the Pennines give way to low-lying countryside, the land is cultivated in any number of ways and there are more towns and villages. The Tees and Wear are often found in deeply entrenched meanders as they flow through the lower parts of County Durham. These areas have been long settled, but only in the past few centuries have they really been tamed.

An ill-defined ridge of magnesian limestone runs along the eastern side of the county, and this soft rock has been cut by a series of steep-sided 'denes', or river valleys, leading to the sea. A

low, rocky cliff-coastline abuts the grey waters of the North Sea, where a lot of coal-spoil was dumped onto the shore in recent decades. A long-running clean-up campaign, called 'Turning the Tide' has restored coastal habitats and transformed the landscape.

An impressive number of villages around County Durham are blessed with extensive central greens, and some villages actually boast several of them. Rather than use the term 'High Street', which is common in many parts of Britain, the term 'Front Street' is almost always used around County Durham.

MINING

County Durham's reserves of lead and coal were mined for centuries, but have now been abandoned. So

Old lead mines can be fascinating, but never be tempted to explore inside them

much reclamation work has been carried out that in some areas it is necessary to look long and hard to realise that mining ever took place there, although many sites have interpretative notices outlining past activities. The general rule, when faced with an opening to an old mine, is to **keep out**. These holes, and the buildings associated with them, are often in a poor state of repair, and prone to collapse when disturbed.

Those who wish to study the mining heritage of Country Durham should visit places such as Killhope, the North of England Lead Mining Museum (Walk 39), and the splendid on-site reconstructions at Beamish (Walk 4). The dedicated Lead Mining Trail runs between Cowshill in Weardale (Walk 39) and Edmundbyers on Derwentside (Walk 40). Several museums have old photographs and exhibits related to mining, as well as splendid displays of minerals amassed over the years.

Coal mining developed through the centuries in County Durham, with simple bell pits giving way to deeper shafts and levels, or to opencast mining, as the machinery became available to allow development of the industry. Former spoil heaps and opencast sites have now been reclaimed, sometimes appearing as rather self-consciously 'new-looking' fields and woodlands. Pit villages still exist, even though their collieries have long since closed – maps point easily to likely sites, with villages called Easington Colliery, Blackhall Colliery,

Trimdon Colliery and so on. Some pit villages may feature a piece of pithead gear as a monument, or there may be housing developments for 'aged miners'. The end of coal mining is literally the end of an era.

RAILWAYS

County Durham is of course the 'cradle of the railways'. Wooden rails were built to facilitate horse-drawn waggons long before iron and steel lines carried steam locomotives. In 1825 George Stephenson's 'Locomotion' hauled itself along the original Stockton & Darlington Railway, and over the next century railways penetrated every nook and cranny of County Durham – tracks crisscrossed the countryside, linking towns and villages. They crossed the high Pennines to transport mineral wealth and stone, spanned deep gorges on lofty viaducts, and pushed their way along the lengths of Teesdale and Weardale. Some routes were dedicated mineral lines, while others carried both freight and passengers.

Ultimately, there was a gradual winding down of passenger services, and as mines and quarries began to close, the railways that served them closed in turn. Tracks were lifted from the trackbeds and everyone believed that the railways had died. However, many of the old trackbeds sprang back to life as railway paths, supplementing the network of footpaths and bridleways running across the countryside, offering traffic-free routes from town

The remains of former industries can be studied while exploring the countryside of County Durham

to town and village to village. Routes were linked to form an impressive network of dedicated railway paths.

The history of the railways is well documented, and there are plenty of sources available for railway enthusiasts. Railway museums in County Durham include the Darlington Railway Centre and Museum, the Timothy Hackworth Victorian and Railway Museum, the Tanfield Railway (which claims to be the oldest operating railway in the world), and Beamish.

ACCESS TO THE COUNTRYSIDE

Most of the routes in this guidebook are on public footpaths, public bridleways, public byways or roads. However, there are also short stretches which are along 'permitted paths', where the owner allows access, but does not intend to dedicate a route as a right of way, and is therefore free to withdraw such access. Some of the railway paths, for instance, are permitted routes. The Boundary Route giving access to the summit of Mickle Fell (Walk 28) is neither a right of way nor a permitted route, but requires an application for a permit. Some walks pass specific heritage sites and museums, where there may be an admission charge for a visit.

The Countryside and Rights of Way Act 2000 resulted in vast areas of the North Pennines being designated as 'open access'. It is important to remember that this access is generally available only on foot, and dogs may not be welcome. Furthermore, land managers are entitled to close access land from time to time, and some areas may be subject to very restricted access, or even no access at all, if there is a compelling need. The latest Ordnance Survey Explorer maps show the full extent of access land, and leaflets showing access land in the North Pennines are produced by the Access and Rights of Way Team at Durham County Council.

Once an area of access land is reached, signs will have been erected at most access points, explaining the nature of the access that is available. If access is being restricted, there should be a notice to that effect, and while you may not be permitted to walk on the access land, rights of way across the land are not affected. If you intend walking on access land, but want to be aware of any restrictions, then it is sensible to check in advance, rather than risk disappointment on the day of your visit. For the Open Access Contact Centre, tel 0300 0602091.

Durham County Council has a very active Countryside Group, whose staff spend a lot of time improving access to the countryside. Council staff may work alongside voluntary groups to clear obstructions from paths, and installing gates, stiles and waymarks to make routes clear and easy to follow. Paths may be re-routed, or permitted paths may be negotiated to allow access to specific features. Rights of way can be inspected at www.durham.gov.uk/prow. Problems

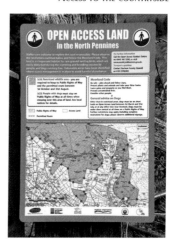

The provision of 'open access' is usually announced by prominent noticeboards at the main access points

encountered around the countryside can be reported to Durham County Council, so that the necessary action can be taken. (Note that Walks 12, 13 and 14 are covered by Darlington Borough Council's Countryside Access Officer, tel 01325 406640.)

The Countryside Group also coordinates and promotes a series of guided walks, exploring all parts of County Durham, throughout the year. These walks are led by countryside rangers and volunteers – the sort of people who tend to have an incredible depth of knowledge – thus allowing visiting walkers the opportunity to enhance their appreciation of the countryside and its heritage.

Durham County Council publishes plenty of information about long and short walks, guided walks, countryside and heritage, which are generally available in leaflet and booklet form. These publications can be found in tourist information centres throughout the county, as well as at some heritage centres and bookshops. Durham County Council's

MAPS

The maps used for the walking routes in this guidebook are extracts from the Ordnance Survey 1:50,000 Landranger Series, which covers County Durham in five sheets. The relevant sheet numbers are 87, 88, 91, 92 and 93. The Ordnance Survey 1:25,000 Explorer Series offers much greater detail, and shows the extent of open access. The relevant sheet numbers are OL19, OL31, 305, 306 and 308.

Detailed cycle route maps can be obtained from Sustrans, the UK's leading sustainable transport charity, www.sustrans.org.uk.

WHAT'S THE WALKING LIKE?

Walking in County Durham is remarkably varied. A low cliff-coast is riven by wooded 'denes', or valleys, so there are plenty of ups and downs along the way. Heading inland, gently rolling countryside becomes progressively hillier, and while some communities are quite charming, other villages and towns

are struggling with their post-industrial identities. Village greens tend to be spacious, and are often used as the starting points for walks into the surrounding countryside.

The western half of County Durham consists of elevated moorlands cleft by broad green dales. Teesdale is without doubt the most scenic, followed closely by Weardale. Walks beside the River Tees and River Wear feature plenty of fine waterfalls, as do their many tributaries, providing powerful displays after prolonged periods of rain. The Pennine Way has introduced many walkers to some of the most outstanding scenery in County Durham, while the Teesdale Way and Weardale Way offer long-distance walks along the two major rivers running through the region.

Wet, windy and misty weather make it difficult to walk on the high moors, so the more elevated routes in this guidebook are best reserved for clear and sunny days, when the scenery can be enjoyed to the full. Some moorland walks are quite popular, but others are quiet, and there may be no other walkers in sight. Those who don't already know the remote parts of County Durham and the bleak and wild North Pennines might be surprised at how unfrequented those places are.

WALKING AND THE WEATHER

No special equipment is needed for the easiest walks in this guidebook.

The short stroll around Durham city is entirely urban, and many other walks are short and simple, seldom straying far from villages. It is sensible to use footwear capable of coping with occasional muddy patches, carrying a waterproof in case of rain, or extra warm clothing in cold weather. On the easier walks, little is needed beyond such bare essentials. If a picnic lunch is needed, it might be possible to buy a snack from a local shop, or enjoy a meal in a pub or restaurant if one is available.

When the walks are longer and harder, heading higher onto remote moorlands, it is necessary to carry more things for safety's sake. Winter can be truly arctic in its severity on the high moors, while short daylight hours can make it difficult to complete a long walk before darkness falls. Full protection is needed if bad weather is encountered, and of course navigational skills need to be good. Poor visibility and dodgy navigation conspire to cause disaster on the high moors, and if things go wrong, it could mean spending a cold and uncomfortable night in the open. Sometimes, it is prudent to wear and carry extra warm clothing, and take extra food and even a basic bivouac.

Deep snow may be rare these days, but when it forms soft drifts and obliterates paths and tracks, progress can be reduced to a crawl, and there is a likelihood that your walk might run into the night. On the other hand, a severe frost can freeze even the boggiest moorlands, enabling walkers to move at a cracking pace in places where time might normally be lost dodging around wet and boggy areas.

TOURIST INFORMATION AND VISITOR CENTRES

Tourist information centres are to be found spread around County Durham. They enable visitors to find out about local services, such as accommodation, public transport and visitor attractions, and many offer plenty of background information, including locally relevant maps, guides, booklets and leaflets. Some centres will be able to assist with accommodation bookings, and all are staffed by people with an excellent working knowledge of local facilities.

Durham City,
tel 03000 262626,
www.thisisdurham.com

Seaham,
Visitor Information,
Dalton Park

Barnard Castle,
Information Point,
The Witham, Horsemarket

Sedgefield,
Visitor Information,
Hardwick Park

Bishop Auckland,
tel 01388 743750,
www.aucklandproject.org

A vintage tram runs through the museum grounds at Beamish (Walk 4)

Stanhope,
tel 01388 527650,
www.durhamdalescentre.co.uk

More specific 'themed' information is available at a number of dedicated visitor centres around County Durham. These are often more than simply museums, as they give the interested visitor a deeper understanding of the history and heritage of the area. Some centres encourage a direct, hands-on approach to their exhibits, featuring working displays. A selection of the main visitor centres, attractions and museums is listed below.

Durham Cathedral,
tel 0191 3868669,
www.durhamcathedral.co.uk

Beamish Museum,
tel 0191 3704000,
www.beamish.org.uk

Head of Steam,
Darlington Railway Museum,
tel 01325 405060,
www.head-of-steam.co.uk

Killhope Museum,
tel 01388 537505,
killhope.org.uk.

Bowlees Visitor Centre,
tel 01833 622145,
www.northpennines.org.uk/
bowlees-visitor-centre

Weardale Museum,
tel 01388 335085,
weardalemuseum.org.uk

Bowes Museum,
tel 01833 690606,
www.thebowesmuseum.org.uk

EMERGENCIES

It is essential that walkers embarking on these routes wear appropriate clothing and footwear, not only for the nature of the terrain, but also with an eye on the day's weather. On the easier walks, it should be a simple matter to abandon the enterprise if the weather is truly awful, or if some minor accident happens. On the more remote walks, bailing out of a difficult situation is not so easy, and assistance might not be readily available. If the emergency services are required at any point, the police, ambulance, fire service, coastguard or mountain rescue can all be contacted by dialling 999 (or the European emergency number 112). The Teesdale and Weardale Search and Mountain Rescue Team operate throughout County Durham, not just on the high moors. Be sure to give them your number so that they can keep in touch with you, and be ready to give them all the information they require so that they can make an appropriate response. Better still, take care not to get into a difficult or dangerous situation in the first place!

The route from High to Low Coniscliffe passes a few isolated farms spread among broad fields (Walk 13)

HOW TO USE THIS GUIDEBOOK

This guidebook contains details of 40 walking routes, spread over all parts of County Durham. Most of them are circular, so that anyone using a car can return to it at the end of their walk, but a few routes are linear and require the use of public transport to complete. Together, these routes cover 510km (317 miles) across immensely rich and varied countryside, taking in some of the finest and most interesting features around the county.

Read the route descriptions carefully before setting out, and if carrying Ordnance Survey maps in addition to the extracts used in this book, be sure to take the ones listed for each walk. The essential information for each route is given under the following headings:

- **Distance** Given in km and miles
- **Terrain** Summary of the nature of the terrain and paths used
- **Start/finish** Usually the same place, but sometimes different
- **Maps** OS Landranger and OS Explorer sheet numbers
- **Refreshments** Summary of pubs and cafés on the route
- **Transport** Basic bus frequency and destinations.

Enjoy your choice of walks and always follow the Country Code.

The Dene Mouth near Peterlee is visited on Walk 7 and Walk 8

WALK 1

Durham City and the River Wear

Start/Finish	Durham Cathedral – GR 273 422
Distance	5km (3 miles)
Terrain	Easy, low-level urban paths, tracks and roads
Maps	OS Landranger 88; Explorer 308
Refreshments	Plenty of pubs, cafés and restaurants around the city
Transport	Durham is a major transport hub, with plenty of bus and rail services. The Cathedral Bus serves the city centre regularly from the railway station and coach park, except Sundays.

Situated on a wooded promontory rising above a deeply entrenched meander of the River Wear, Durham city is redolent with history and stirs the spirit. The Dunholme – the hill crowned with the cathedral, castle and college – is a designated world heritage site. Before exploring the county of Durham, it is well worth exploring the city. Wander through the poky alleyways around Market Place before striding along both banks of the River Wear – no one leaves Durham city disappointed. This simple stroll could be accomplished in as little as an hour, but with 1000 years of accumulated history to see, it could take as much as a week!

A viewing platform was added to the tower in 2019.

Starting at **Durham Cathedral**, the best climb in the city is up the 325 steps of the central tower – weather and opening times permitting. ◄ You can look down on this short day's walk, as well as across country to distant hills and the moors of the North Pennines.

Descend from the tower, leave the cathedral and walk round Palace Green, passing the college and castle. Follow a narrow road down to **Market Place**. Turn left to continue down narrow, cobbled Silver Street, which is lined with shops, to reach **Framwellgate Bridge**. Cross the bridge and descend a flight of steps on the left, beside a pub. Turn right to walk upstream beside the **River Wear** and enjoy fine views across to the

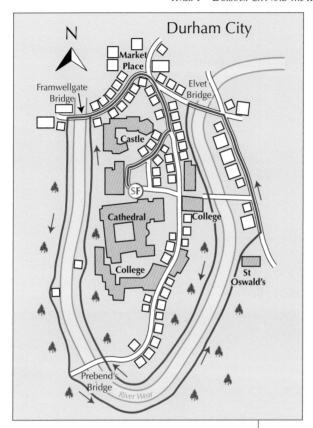

castle and cathedral. The path passes a weir on its way to **Prebend's Bridge**. Don't cross the bridge, but maybe take photographs from its parapet, and read Sir Walter Scott's words carved in stone.

Beyond Prebend's Bridge, the broad path drifts from the river and later climbs up a wooded slope to reach **St Oswald's Church**. Bear left to leave the churchyard, which is managed as a wildflower meadow, and walk along Church Street and New Elvet, turning left to cross **Elvet Bridge**.

Descend via steps from the bridge to reach the riverside path and head downstream. The path runs below some of the colleges and passes under modern Kingsgate Bridge. Proceed through the entrenched meander of the River Wear and then beneath Prebend's Bridge to reach the Old Fuller's Mill, which stands beside the weir passed in the early stages of the walk. Framwellgate Bridge lies further along the path, where you can climb back up into the city and visit any places that caught your attention earlier.

Durham City celebrated its millennium in 1995, recalling the day in 995 when the congregation of St Cuthbert brought their founder's body onto the Dunholme – the wooded promontory rising above a crook in the River Wear. The rest, as they say, is history. Rather than attempt to distil 1000 years of history onto half a page here, those who want to know more should get hold of the colourful,

The stout stone towers of Durham Cathedral completely dominate the skyline of Durham city

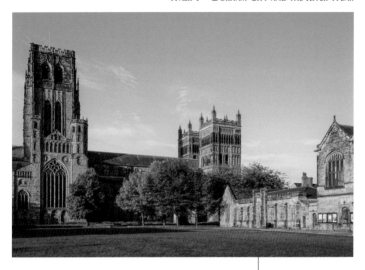

condensed, informative booklet *Durham – 1000 Years of History* by Martin Roberts, published by The History Press. Many of Durham city's main attractions have plenty of their own background material. Visit the Durham Museum www.durham-museum.co.uk.

Durham Cathedral rises above the spacious Palace Green

WALK 2

Bearpark, Broompark and Brandon

Start/Finish	Deerness Gymnastics Academy, Ushaw Moor – GR 236 423
Distance	12km (7½ miles)
Terrain	Easy, low-level field paths and old railway trackbeds
Maps	OS Landranger 88; Explorer 308
Refreshments	Pubs at Bearpark and Brandon, or off-route at Broompark and Ushaw Moor
Transport	Regular daily buses serve Ushaw Moor, Bearpark, Broompark and Brandon from Durham city

Ushaw Moor lies just to the west of Durham city. Dispel any notions of a moorland walk, as the area is well cultivated and well settled. The starting point is a leisure centre and the route visits the villages of Bearpark, Broompark and Brandon. There are short stretches of railway paths, including the junction of the Lanchester Valley Way, Deerness Valley Way and Brandon to Bishop Auckland Way. The route explores the valleys of the River Browney and River Deerness, with the ruins of Beaurepaire seen in the early stages. Views are occasionally wide-ranging, with Durham Cathedral often popping up as a reference point.

Leave the Deerness Gymnastics Academy near Ushaw Moor, following a road behind it by turning left. The road then bends right as it passes through a housing estate. Don't take any roads to left or right, but watch for a bridleway sign on the left before reaching **Broom Hall**. A clear path leaves the estate to run northwards through fields. Cross a gentle rise to reach the village of **Bearpark** facing its parish church.

Turn left to walk up the road, passing a couple of shops, take-aways, a pub and bus stops. Watch for a bridleway sign on the right, buried in foliage, opposite a school gate in the upper part of the village. Walk along a road, then branch left along a tarmac path through a grassy area. Follow this path straight down to a road and cross it.

Continue down through a housing estate, where the path simply cuts between the houses. At the bottom, turn right along a track and follow it to a road. Turn left to walk down the road, which becomes a dirt road that crosses an old railway trackbed, called the Lanchester Valley Way. Either turn right to follow it, or consider a short detour to nearby **Beaurepaire** ('Bearpark (remains of)' on the map).

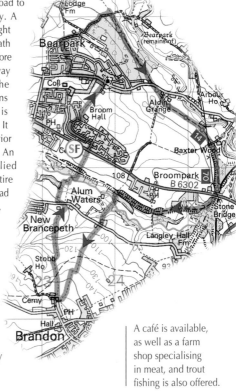

For the detour, which is quite short, continue down the dirt road to cross the River Browney. A gate and stile on the right give access to a short path climbing to the ruins. Explore and return to the railway trackbed to resume the walk. **Beaurepaire** means 'beautiful retreat' and is contracted as Bearpark. It was built in 1258 for Prior Bertram de Middleton. An extensive estate supplied food and fuel for the entire household. Beaurepaire had living areas, a large hall, kitchen, chapel, and so on, making it a self-contained unit. Nearby Aldin Grange was attached to the manor as a farm.

Follow the Lanchester Valley Way, which overlooks the valley of the River Browney and crosses a road near Aldin Grange. ▶

A café is available, as well as a farm shop specialising in meat, and trout fishing is also offered.

37

The ruins of Beaurepaire can be visited by detouring slightly off route

The trackbed features a link with Durham city and runs close to the main line railway at a point where a road bridge crosses it. Two more railway trackbed walks branch apart ahead. Keep straight ahead along the Deerness Valley Railway Path, which runs through the **Broompark** picnic area.

> The Broompark picnic area includes the junction of the **Lanchester Valley Way**, **Deerness Valley Way** and the **Brandon to Bishop Auckland Way**. These have been developed from old railway trackbeds. The line through the Lanchester Valley carried ironstone from the Cleveland Hills to steelworks at Consett. The line through the Deerness Valley to Bishop Auckland mainly carried coal, linking nine collieries. It crossed the valley on a huge timber viaduct, now long dismantled. The railways closed in the 1960s and have been converted to multi-use railway paths.

Walk along an embankment and through a cutting. As you leave the cutting, look out for a gate down to the left, where a footpath drops down steps. ▶ Walk down to the wooded banks of the River Deerness, crossing two footbridges before the path leads up to Primrose Side Farm, passing between buildings, then cross a road.

An obvious path is signposted running straight uphill from the farm, climbing at a gentle gradient. Watch carefully for waymarks, turning right and left round the edge of a field at a higher level. The path leads to the edge of the village of **Brandon**, where a right turn leads to the first few houses. The Pub & Kitchen lies up to the left, but if this isn't being visited, then turn right downhill to continue.

A path leaves the road as signposted between two houses and leads back into fields. The descent is fairly clear, but watch for helpful waymarks on the stiles that need to be used. Cross straight over a track along the way, rather than following it. The route leads down into a small valley to cross a runnel of water. A slight climb over a rise in the fields leads to the roadside near Unthank Farm between New Brancepeth and **Alum Waters**.

An obvious short-cut can be made by following the trackbed onwards, turning right to finish.

A track rises past fields to reach the edge of the village of Brandon

Turn left along a road to pass the farm, then right to walk down an enclosed track. Bear right at the end of the track and cross a footbridge over the River Deerness. Climb straight uphill, crossing the Deerness Valley Way, and follow a path up through fields to reach the Deerness Gymnastics Academy where the walk started.

WALK 3
Dipton and Hamsterley Mill

Start/Finish	Collierley Primary School, Dipton – GR 152 535
Distance	9km (5½ miles)
Terrain	Easy field paths and woodland paths, but vague at times
Maps	OS Landranger 88; Explorer 307
Refreshments	Café and takeaways at Dipton
Transport	Regular daily buses serve Dipton and Hamsterley from Newcastle and Consett

A charming patchwork of fields, mixed woodlands and forest lies between the hilltop village of Dipton and the valley village of Hamsterley Mill. This short walk descends from Dipton, through fields and woods, to reach a short stretch of the Derwent Walk, based on an old railway trackbed running from Consett to Swalwell. The return journey climbs through fields and forest before following a charming wooded valley up to Pontop Hall. Views from the fields around Dipton stretch all around Derwentside, while Pontop Pike is easily spotted because its summit bears a prominent array of tall masts.

Start in **Dipton** at Collierley Primary School and walk down the A692 through the village. Turn left at the Scout and Guide building and follow a road that becomes a track descending alongside allotments. Go down through fields until a stile appears on the right. Cross the stile and head straight across sloping fields, passing tall trees on the way to other stiles. Cross the access road above **Collierley Farm** then follow the path through an area of scrub. ▶ Cross a small stream in a wooded ravine and walk across the next open field. Turn left down a grassy track from a gate.

There are signs that this used to be a railway trackbed.

Walk down to and enter **Ewehurst Wood**, to follow a clear path through it. Exit from the wood, turn right and follow the woodland edge. Turn left to follow the access road to **Low Ewehurst**. Keep well to the right of the farm buildings to cross a stile giving access to fields. Again, follow the woodland edge and walk to the far end of

The woods on both sides of the road are managed by the Woodland Trust, who allow free access.

the fields. A gate leads into more woods and a path runs downhill. Cross a footbridge to reach the B6310. ◄

Cross the road and climb two flights of steps. Turn left along a path, then left again along an old railway trackbed, which is the Derwent Valley Way. Cross a bridge, then cross the B6310 road beside **Hamsterley Mill**. Continue along the old railway trackbed, which now serves as a walking route and cycleway also designated as Sustrans route 14. Follow it beneath a stone-arch bridge near High Hamsterley.

At this point a 2km (1¼ mile) detour is recommended to the **Derwentcote Steel Furnace**, as follows. Continue along the trackbed through the woods, crossing a road to continue along an embankment. Watch for a path down to the right, from a bench, to the A694. Cross the road and walk down Forge Lane to find the old furnace.

Derwentcote Steel Furnace was an early steelworks, built in the 1730s, pre-dating Bessemer furnaces. Each 'cementation' cycle took three weeks to complete, with maximum temperatures of 1100°C, producing 10 tons of steel. Derwentside was the centre of the British steel industry in the early 18th century, but Derwentcote was out of use by 1891. Nearby Consett developed a huge steel-works, now a mere memory.

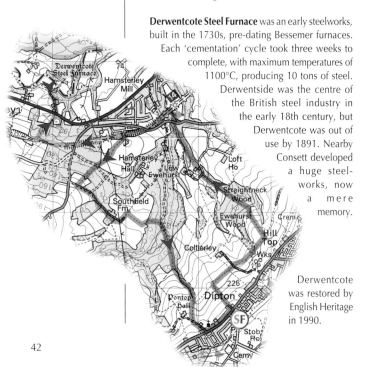

Derwentcote was restored by English Heritage in 1990.

The walk leaves the Derwent Valley Way at a stout stone arch

Staying on the main route, climb up steps beside the stone-arch bridge near High Hamsterley. At the top, follow a right of way through a field. Keep left of a prominent pylon in the rushy field beyond and continue to an indented corner in the forest beyond. A gate gives access to the forest, where you turn left along a track, then keep straight ahead along a path. The path climbs gently and leaves the forest to hit a farm access road. Turn left to walk to **Southfield Farm**. Go slightly left while walking through the farmyard to locate a clear track leading into the fields.

The track suddenly turns left and ends at a gate. Turn right to follow a hedgerow, then head left to reach a stile giving access to Collierley Wood. Follow a boardwalk path downhill and turn right to cross a bridge over Pont Burn. A track climbs up through the woods parallel to Pikewell Burn. At a higher level, another path crosses from right to left. Turn left along it, then almost immediately turn right to continue uphill. Leave the woods later to join an access road near **Pontop Hall**. Turn left to walk up to a church in Dipton, then left along the main road to finish.

Dipton is essentially a late-19th-century mining village, which once had its own link with the railway network. However, there were buildings in the area long before the development of the village.

WALK 4

Beamish and Causey

Start/Finish	Eden Place picnic area, Beamish – GR 218 537
Distance	10km (6¼ miles)
Terrain	Easy, low-level paths and tracks through fields and woodlands
Maps	OS Landranger 88; Explorer 308
Refreshments	Pub at Beamish; pubs and café at Causey
Transport	Regular daily buses serve Beamish and Causey from Newcastle, Chester-le-Street and Consett

The Living Museum of the North at Beamish is a reconstruction and celebration of everyday life in the early 19th and 20th centuries. The museum has been developing since 1971 and visitors need a whole day to explore it properly. This route completely encircles the museum and passes Beamish Hall on the way to Causey Arch. The earliest years of the Industrial Revolution can be investigated in the wooded valley spanned by Causey Arch. The Tanfield Railway passes nearby, so steam trains may be an added attraction. Older walkers may find the route tinged with nostalgia, while younger walkers may view things with a mixture of wonder and puzzlement. When both walk together in this area, there are splendid opportunities to share information and experiences.

Read the notice explaining about the shepherd and shepherdess figures above the inn entrance.

The Eden Place picnic area is close to the main entrance to the Living Museum of the North at **Beamish**. Walk almost to the museum entrance, which is dominated by a massive steam hammer. Turn right and left to pass the Shepherd and Shepherdess Inn ◀ and follow a minor road down towards **High Forge**. Turn left along an enclosed path beside a house, cross a track and follow a stone-paved path downhill. As this runs through the museum complex, and you haven't paid to enter, please stay on the right of way. Notice a rebuilt church to the left, and walk up to a farmyard, continuing straight through. Bear right to follow a track through gates, dropping to Beamish Burn.

The walk starts and finishes near an imposing steam hammer at the entrance to the museum at Beamish

Cross this little river then follow it upstream using a field path. There is a good riverside path at first, but it gets better later. As you follow the path through woods further along, there are tantalising views of the reconstructed museum buildings – enough to ensure a return visit to learn more.

Turn left along a prominent track in the woods and follow it further upstream alongside Beamish Burn to reach the entrance to **Beamish Hall**. Turn right and left by road alongside a tall boundary wall. Later, at a crossroads
▶ turn right and walk up a broad track at **Coppy**, signposted for Causey Arch. The track passes between fields and gradually narrows. Turn left along a broad track, then right along a narrower track before emerging onto a road at **Causey**. Turn right to reach the Beamish Park

Note The Stables micro-brewery down to the left.

45

Hotel and Causey Arch Inn, then left downhill to cross the busy A6076. Cross a level-crossing and turn left into the Causey Arch car park, where the Causey House Tea Rooms are available.

A path from the car park leads into a wooded gorge. A choice of paths is signposted – one going down into the gorge and crossing footbridges before climbing to Causey Arch – one staying high above the gorge to proceed more directly to Causey Arch – and another running parallel to the Tanfield Railway. The latter two routes can be extended past a replica wooden coal waggon to reach a viewpoint. Whichever way is chosen to reach **Causey Arch**, spend a while marvelling at its graceful and aged span – the oldest surviving single-span railway arch in the world.

'Carrying coals to Newcastle' sums up the reason for **Causey Arch**'s existence. As collieries near Newcastle became exhausted, those in the surrounding countryside became more active to fulfil demand, but a problem lay in transporting the coal from country to city. Horse-power reigned supreme in the 18th century, and heavily laden waggons hauled over heavily used tracks led to severe erosion, slower passage times, and a higher cost to the consumer. Horses were only able to haul heavy waggons up gentle gradients, so steep slopes had to be bypassed or crossed by bridges. Specially constructed 'waggonways' were laid, with wooden rails for the wooden wheels of waggons, and transport became smoother and faster. Causey Arch was constructed in 1725 to overcome severe gradients

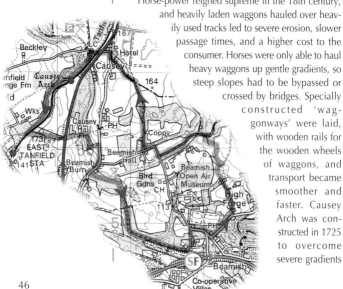

near the Tanfield collieries. An explosion at one of the Tanfield mines quickly led to the closure of the site in the 1740s. Traffic across Causey Arch slowed to a trickle and ceased altogether in 1786.

The Tanfield Railway operates past Causey Arch on this walk

Walkers using the lower path should climb to the top of the arch, but without crossing it. Walkers using the higher paths should cross the arch. Now that everyone is on the same track, proceed towards the head of Causey Burn. A path on the left is signposted 'Top of Causey Gorge'. Enjoy following this old waggonway through the woods, but be sure to cross the footbridge over Causey Burn when it finally appears. Bear left after crossing the footbridge, then carefully cross the **Tanfield Railway**.

The embankment used by the **Tanfield Railway** was once a waggonway, and one of many in the area. It was used by horse-drawn traffic in 1725, then static winding engines were installed in the 1830s. By the 1880s, steam engines and a regular railway came onto the scene. The line operated until 1962, but not long after closure it was revived as a tourist attraction. The line currently runs from Sunniside to East Tanfield. Given its early start and gradual transition from horses to locomotives, the Tanfield Railway claims to be the world's oldest operating railway. Tel 07508 092365, www.tanfield-railway.co.uk.

After crossing the line, a field path climbs over a rise and descends to the busy **A6076**. Cross the road and follow another waymarked path past **Causey Hall**, then go over Causey Burn again. A right turn leads through former Causey Mill **picnic area**. Follow an access road uphill, then turn right down a minor road and cross a bridge over the river.

Climb uphill, and either pass through a large gateway, or a narrow doorway, in the tall boundary wall on the left side of the road. Follow the most obvious path through the woods. Be sure to bear right later, and follow a path running uphill to enter a woodland managed by the Woodland Trust. Later, pass straight through a cross-track. The track that runs uphill later bends left, leading back through woods to return to the Eden Place picnic area. Note that an old railway trackbed runs parallel to the track to Eden Place, designated as Sustrans route 7.

After decades of growth, the **Living Museum of the North** at Beamish has proved to be a major tourist attraction. Coach-loads of visitors and educational groups arrive to study the daily living conditions of the early 19th and 20th centuries. This is a world of trams, vintage motors, steam trains, oil lamps and open coal fires. Life at home and at work, out shopping, in the pub or at the chapel, is all authentically reconstructed. A replica coalmine stands alongside actual buildings that have been removed stone by stone and brick by brick from their original locations and painstakingly reconstructed on site. At busy times there are plenty of people in period costume, with brass bands playing and traditional sporting activities taking place. It's a great place for grandparents to take their grandchildren. Simply follow the signs and be prepared to stay all day. Tel 0191 3704000, www.beamish.org.uk.

WALK 5
Ouston and Urpeth

Start/Finish	St Benet's School, Ouston – GR 256 541
Distance	7km (4 miles)
Terrain	Easy low-level paths and tracks through fields and woodlands
Maps	OS Landranger 88; Explorer 308
Refreshments	Pub and a couple of shops in Ouston
Transport	Ouston is served by regular daily buses from Chester-le-Street and Newcastle

Ouston and Urpeth Conservation Volunteers (OUCV) have waymarked a short circular walk as part of Durham County Council's Parish Paths Partnership. The route also lies within the Great North Forest. Easy field paths and farm tracks, along with riverside and woodland paths, have been highlighted using eye-catching 'ladybird' waymarks. The area is surprisingly rich in wildlife, despite being in clear view of urban Gateshead. The local conservation volunteers also manage a nursery to generate a constant supply of plants that are used to grace flowerbeds in the area.

St Benet's School is on the southern edge of Ouston, where St Benet's Way branches off the main road. A 'mushroom' sculpture stands near the road junction and marks the starting point. Walk along a grassy verge beside St Benet's Way, then turn left at a gate to follow a grassy track through fields. This passes a mobile phone mast and continues towards prominent Urpeth Hall.

Turn left along a road to pass farm buildings behind Urpeth Hall. As the road runs downhill, turn right and cross a stile, then walk straight through a field. Cross another stile and follow a path with steps

The River Team is crossed between Riding Farm and Urpeth

into a wooded valley. The **River Team** leads downstream from woods into a meadow. Cross a flat bridge later and continue along the foot of a wooded slope.

The path eventually climbs from the valley and a track leads to a road. Turn right to follow the road towards **Riding Farm**, then turn right again down a track. A bridge crosses the River Team again and climbs to a road near the dormitory estate of **Urpeth**.

Turn left down the road, then right, with views of tower blocks in nearby Gateshead. When the road reaches a dip, turn right through a gap in a hedge into a field. Head towards Walter's Wood and cross a tiny stream in an easy stride to pick up a path on the other side.

The path runs up through a pleasant, mature beech wood in a small valley couched between Ouston and Urpeth. When a tarmac path is reached, keep straight ahead until forced to make a choice, then turn left and keep straight ahead until houses are reached on the edge of **Ouston**.

On reaching these houses, turn right along a grassy path, then walk beside back-garden fences to return to St Benet's Way. Turn left to finish back at St Benet's School. Turn left again if you want to walk into Ouston to visit the pub or catch a bus.

WALK 6

Lumley Castle and Great Lumley

Start/Finish	Chester-le-Street – GR 274 516
Distance	11.5km (7 miles)
Terrain	Easy low-level paths and tracks through fields, woods and beside rivers
Maps	OS Landranger 88; Explorer 308
Refreshments	Plenty of choice around Chester-le-Street; pub and takeaway at Great Lumley
Transport	Regular daily buses serve Chester-le-Street from Newcastle, Durham and Consett. Regular daily buses link Great Lumley and Chester-le-Street. Some trains between Durham and Newcastle stop at Chester-le-Street.

Lumley Castle rises across the River Wear from Chester-le-Street. A solid-looking edifice, the castle was founded in the 14th century. It stands on the brow of a low hill and is almost entirely encircled by rivers, forming a natural moat. The Weardale Way follows these rivers, looping round the castle. To gain a little extra distance and explore the country around Lumley Castle in more detail, this loop of the Weardale Way is extended through the village of Great Lumley and down the river to Chester New Bridge, to form a longer circuit. The town of Chester-le-Street can be explored at the beginning or end of the walk.

Start in the centre of Chester-le-Street at GW Horners' pub and follow the road marked 'No Entry', as signposted for the Leisure Centre and Riverside Park. Keep to the right-hand bank to follow Cong Burn to its confluence with the River Wear. Turn right to walk upstream along-side the Wear through Riverside Park. Cross busy Lumley Bridge, then turn immediately left. A short detour up a road offers a glimpse of **Lumley Castle**, but return to fol-low a riverside path beneath the busy road bridge.

Although **Lumley Castle** dates from the 14th century it was largely reworked in 1712. Sir Ralph Lumley founded the castle, but lost it after joining a conspiracy to supplant Henry IV with Richard II. However, the castle later reverted to the family, who remained closely associated with it and the town of Chester-le-Street. The former estate associated with the castle has been broken up and the ground in front of the castle is now a golf course. The castle is now a hotel, with splendid furnishings, specialising in weddings and banquets. See www.lumleycastle.com.

From Lumley Bridge follow a path upstream along the wooded bank of the River Wear. The path later heads uphill, away from the river, and crosses a farm access road. Climb out of the woods and bear right round the edge of a field. The path runs almost to the farm of **Lumley Riding**, where a right turn leads away from the farm beside a long field. At the far end of this field, a left turn leads to a hilltop village.

Follow a minor road straight into **Great Lumley**, passing shops and the Old England pub and the parish church, then pass a school before turning left along another road. Just as the road leaves the village, turn right along a tarmac path and follow it alongside new houses. When a gate and stile are reached, turn left to follow a path across a field, heading straight back to the road.

Walk along the road to cross the **B1284** at a roundabout. A minor road leads down to the former Smith's Arms, then passes beneath a flyover on the A1(M). Immediately on the left, while passing beneath the bridge, climb a flight of steps to cut out a bend in the minor road. Turn left and left again at the top to follow a farm access road.

The farm road continues along to the right of the Manor House and runs down into Lumley Park Wood. The track leads through a richly wooded gorge to a stone bridge. Don't cross the bridge, but look through the trees for the rear of Lumley Castle. Continue along the woodland track, which is heavy with the garlic scent of ramsons in spring. Keep to the right of Garden House, squeezing past on a narrow path. Further along the

A riverside path follows Lumley Park Burn through Lumley Park Wood

A gate in a wall offers seasonal access to woodland walks near Lambton Castle.

woodland path, look out for a clear turning off to the right and climb uphill out of the woods. A field path leads up to a bridge across the A1(M), then a farm access road leads through an impressive gateway onto the **A183**. ◄

Turn left and follow this busy road downhill. Cross over Lambton Bridge, but note the fine view of 14th-century Chester New Bridge. This is one of the access points for nearby Lambton Castle. Cross the road, away from Chester New Bridge, to follow a path running upstream alongside the River Wear. A loop of the river passes beneath the A1(M), before continuing past a sewage works hidden behind a screen of trees. Keep following the riverside path to reach Cong Burn, and turn right to follow it back into Chester-le-Street.

As the name suggests, **Chester-le-Street** was a Roman foundation, and the site of the old Roman fort is partially exposed alongside the Salvation Army building. The main roads that ran through the fort are thought to lie beneath the church of St Mary and St Cuthbert. The church was founded in 883 by monks fleeing Lindisfarne, and was one of many resting places for the body of St Cuthbert. A Saxon cathedral stood on the site and several phases of development can be seen around the building. An interesting annexe called the Anker's House – an anchorite's cell from 1383 to 1547 – is now a small museum. See www.maryandcuthbert.org.uk.

WALK 7
Durham Coast Path

Start	Byron Place, Seaham – GR 431 493
Finish	Hart Station – GR 483 360
Distance	20km (12½ miles)
Terrain	Mostly easy cliff paths and tracks, with some steep paths in wooded valleys
Maps	OS Landrangers 88 and 93; Explorers 306 and 308
Refreshments	Pubs and cafés at Seaham, Easington Colliery, Horden, Blackhall Colliery and Crimdon Dene Coastal Hub
Transport	Regular daily buses serve Seaham from Durham, Sunderland and all points along the coast to and from Hartlepool. Rail services link Seaham with Sunderland and Hartlepool.

Seaham, Dawdon, Easington, Horden and Blackhall had collieries during the 20th century. Miners dug up to 8km (5 miles) out to sea, and spoil from the pits was piled into heaps or tipped onto the shore. All the pits have been closed, the pit-head workings long dismantled, and black ground has given way to green. The cliff-coast is formed from crumbling magnesian limestone cut by interesting wooded valleys (or 'denes'). The National Trust, under its Operation Neptune campaign, acquired stretches of the Durham coast, and in partnership with local authorities and other agencies, delivered the highly successful millennium project 'Turning the Tide', which restored coastal habitats and transformed the landscape. The Durham Coast Path stretches from Seaham to Hart Station, along a designated heritage coast, durhamheritagecoast.org, now incorporated into the England Coast Path.

Lord Byron had an unhappy time at **Seaham**, which was a farming settlement in 1815. He married briefly into the Milbanke family and wrote to a friend: 'Upon this dreary coast we have nothing but county meetings and shipwrecks; and I have this day dined upon fish, which probably dined

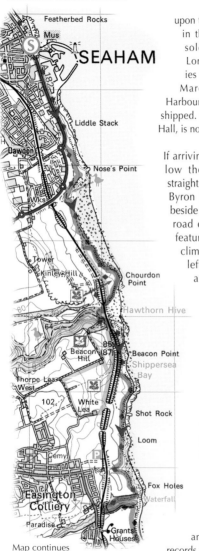

upon the crews of several colliers lost in the late gales.' The Milbankes sold land to the Marquess of Londonderry, and three collieries were opened in the area. The Marquess constructed Seaham Harbour in 1828 to enable coal to be shipped. Byron's former home, Seaham Hall, is now a luxury hotel and spa.

If arriving in Seaham by train, simply follow the signposted pedestrian route straight from the station towards the coast. Byron Place is a shopping development beside the main coast road, or A182. This road overlooks **Seaham Harbour**, and features a footpath and cycleway as it climbs gently uphill to leave town. Turn left at a road junction where there are coastal footpath signposts and walk past a cliff-top car park on the site of an old colliery. There is a trodden path on the grassy slope beside the road. With care, a view over the crumbling cliff edge reveals a slender pinnacle of rock, the **Liddle Stack**, rising from the beach. Continue onwards to reach **Nose's Point**.

The Marquess of Londonderry had a shaft sunk here for **Dawdon Colliery** in 1899 and coal was raised in 1907. There were several seams of coal, with the deepest sinkings reaching 520m (1700ft). The pit employed 20,000 people, and broke British and European records for coal production in the 1970s.

Map continues on page 58

Problems were experienced soon afterwards and production ceased in 1991. Spoil from the mine was dumped on the beach, where the sea spread it along the coast, so that the magnesian limestone sea-cliffs are now effectively marooned inland. The landscaped cliff-tops have been transformed into wildflower meadows.

Follow the coast path across a footbridge and look back along Blast Beach. Views stretch all the way along the Durham coast, which stops short of the smoky chimneys of industrial Teesmouth, with the North York Moors rising beyond. Boulby Cliff, the highest cliff on the east coast of England, might also be seen.

Follow the clearly marked coastal path around **Chourdon Point**, then there is a choice of routes. One involves a steep descent to the beach at **Hawthorn Hive**. The other is gentler, but involves crossing the railway line with care, then soon afterwards turning left down a path to cross the well-wooded **Hawthorn Burn**.

The wooded **dene** (valley) leading inland to the village of Hawthorn was landscaped in the 19th century by the Pemberton family, who lived at

Hawthorn Towers, now long demolished. Durham Wildlife Trust manages the land and Hawthorn Dene Meadows features up to 100 species of wild flowers. A soaring brick railway arch was built in 1905, and on the other side of it is Hawthorn Hive – a 'hive' is a landing place for boats. The valley mouth is choked with sea-washed colliery spoil, but cod, plaice and whiting, as well as bass and wrasse, swim close to the shore, and seals and porpoises have also been spotted.

Cross the footbridge and follow a broad path uphill, turning left after passing the ruins of a brick hut. The path leads through the southernmost arch of the railway viaduct. ◀ The coast path again follows the railway southwards, passing through rich grasslands with views of the cliffs at **Beacon Point**. Drift away from the railway to follow a good stretch of the cliff path. This passes the site of **Easington Colliery**, where vast amounts of spoil were once dumped onto the shore by conveyor belt.

The path climbing from the beach joins here.

Easington Colliery can be visited by heading inland through a railway arch. A shaft was sunk in 1899 and coal was raised by 1909. Huts were replaced by houses and the area prospered through the 20th century. Disaster struck in 1951 when an explosion in the mine killed 81 miners. Later 81 trees were planted in their memory. Mine shafts extended for 8km (5 miles) out to sea, and the collieries at Easington, Horden and Blackhall were connected by emergency shafts.

Map continues on page 60

58

Looking back towards Nose's Point and Dawdon along the coast path

Easington Colliery finally closed in 1993, leaving social deprivation in its wake. ▶

Follow a tarmac path in a loop around the cliffs, passing alongside Fox Holes Dene to reach another railway arch. The path leads back towards the cliffs, and while looking across the dene a host of little 'fox holes' can be seen on the far side.

The National Trust launched **Operation Neptune** to highlight threats to the coast, securing and safeguarding scenic stretches. The emphasis was not on preserving the coast, but actively restoring it to its natural state after the decades of destruction wreaked by the coal industry. The underlying magnesian limestone allows a rich variety of wild flowers to become established. ▶

The site of **Horden Colliery** is passed and the coastal path moves inland three times as it crosses three little denes. There are steps in places and the path is easy enough to follow. After crossing Blackhalls Gill, the coastal grasslands were regenerated under the Countryside Stewardship scheme. The cliff path leads onwards and cuts inland just before Castle Eden Dene, descending via steps to reach a narrow road. Follow the road down to a small car park and continue walking down towards the beach. Turn right to cross broad **Dene**

Easington village stood in for the fictional village of Everington in the film Billy Elliot. There are plenty of shops.

Horden Point was the 800th kilometre (500th mile) of coast to be brought under the Trust's protection.

59

Mouth, following a track through scrub-covered shingle and marsh to cross a bridge.

The Dene Mouth lies at the foot of **Castle Eden Dene**, which is the broadest and longest of the eight denes on the Durham coast. The area was originally salt marsh, but was overwhelmed by accumulated waste from nearby collieries. Exploration inland, beyond the prominent 10-arched railway viaduct, can be made by following Walk 8.

Pass the end of a road and use a flight of stout concrete steps to climb back onto the cliffs, where the coast path moves onwards. The site of **Blackhall Colliery** is passed later.

A shaft was sunk here for **Blackhall Colliery** in 1909, and the first miners lived in huts or even tents on the beach, since houses could not be built fast enough for them. The mine was notoriously wet and difficult to work, closing in 1981. Land was reclaimed in 1987 and planted with trees, but the soil is thin and the trees are struggling.

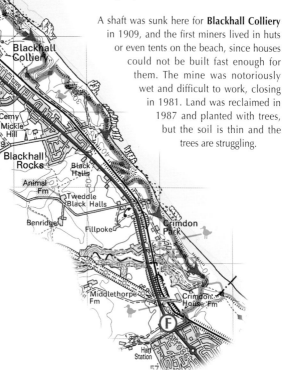

Follow the path inland to the head of Blue House Gill. On reaching the head of the gill, follow a path back towards the coast. A good stretch of coastal path continues, reaching a road-end viewpoint at Blackhall Rocks.

Continue along the cliff path, but note that one stretch is pushed inland a little, then later a couple of steep-sided denes have to be negotiated, using steps and paths that head inland for a while. Just as a railway arch is reached, the path returns to the coast to pass mobile homes at **Crimdon Park**.

A blaze of gorse bushes on the coast between Horden and Blackhall Colliery

A tea hut was established on **Crimdon Banks** in 1921, followed by a variety of huts and tents. The local council acquired land in 1935 and a pub, fairground and paddling pool were established. Crimdon Lido became known as the 'Holiday Resort of Many Happy Returns', and the Miss Crimdon competitions were a highlight of the summer months.

Follow the coast path along the low cliffs at Crimdon Dene Holiday Park ▶ and then continue down a road to the mouth of Crimdon Dene. Cross a bridge and walk up a go straight up a clear path, through a gate, to cross a footbridge over the railway at former **Hart Station**. Pass the old station building to reach a road, then turn right and left by road to reach bus stops on the main A1086. Buses can be caught back to Seaham, or ahead to Hartlepool, which has a railway station.

The Crimdon Dene Coastal Hub and Dunes café opened in 2022.

WALK 8

Castle Eden Dene

Start/Finish	Horden – GR 440 409
Distance	13.5km (8½ miles)
Terrain	Mostly easy wooded paths and tracks, with some steep stretches
Maps	OS Landrangers 88 and 93; Explorer 308
Refreshments	Shops and takeaways at Horden; café at Oakerside Dene Lodge
Transport	Regular daily buses from Durham, Sunderland, Hartlepool and Peterlee cross Castle Eden Dene, but buses only stop at Horden

Of the eight wooded denes (or valleys) that lead down to the Durham coast, **Castle Eden Dene** is the longest, deepest and most accessible. This richly wooded valley is managed as a national nature reserve, and although there is only one right of way crossing it, a splendid network of paths allows a thorough exploration. This route starts where the main road crosses the dene near Horden. There is only a single access track at first, then more paths appear, allowing walkers to climb up to Castle Eden village and continue round the head of the dene. The return route is along the northern slopes, and once the main road is reached, an extension leads to the Dene Mouth.

Castle Eden Dene boasts ancient woodland, reckoned to be a remnant of the original 'wildwood' that once covered Britain – there are plenty of very old yews, along with sturdy oaks and wych elms. The understorey contains holly, hazel, hawthorn, blackthorn, alder and wild rose, and ground cover features ivy, bluebells and rampant ramsons. Invasive sycamore grows in the lower reaches. Two main roads and a railway cut across the dene, and the Durham coast path crosses the Dene Mouth. Dense foliage dampens the noise of traffic, so birdsong is more likely to be heard on this walk. The soft magnesian limestone is covered with boulder clay, so landslips are common, and allowed to regenerate naturally. The northern brown argus butterfly can be spotted around the dene.

Start from Horden and walk down the A1086 as if going to Blackhall. A gateway on the right gives access to Castle Eden Dene and a national nature reserve sign stands alongside. Follow a broad tarmac path down into the wooded dene, running close to **Castle Eden Burn** from time to time. Eventually, the track crosses humpbacked Garden of Eden Bridge. Not far beyond the bridge, turn left to follow a zigzag path uphill.

Don't leave the woods at the top of this path, but turn right to follow a path just inside the woodland fence. The path stays high on the southern edge of Castle Eden Dene and is known as Miss Mary's Walk. The path loops round a small side-valley, then later runs downhill and reaches a broader track.

Turn left to follow the broad track uphill and exit from the woodland at a prominent gateway near St James' Church. After passing through the gateway, turn immediately right to go through another gateway. An access road leads towards the fine old house of **Castle Eden**, then the woods are entered again at another gate beyond.

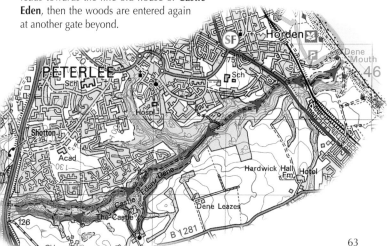

A fine woodland path rises towards Castle Eden

The manor of **Castle Eden** is ancient, but the current layout of the estate – castle, church and village – dates from the mid-18th century. The Burdon family, whose male heirs were always called Rowland, developed the area into the mid-20th century. The Nimmo family was also associated with the estate. They were brewers, and produced Castle Eden Ale, although their brewery was far removed from the village.

Turn left once inside the woods and continue along a path near the top edge. Later, the path begins to drop downhill and reaches a humpbacked bridge called Gunners Pool Bridge. You could cross this bridge over a deep gorge and shorten the walk, or, without crossing the bridge, continue along the path towards the head of the dene. If continuing, note that the path drops again and crosses two footbridges in close succession, the second one being off to the left. The path then runs uphill, close to the edge of the woods again, until another path leads off to the right down a flight of steps. Cross a footbridge spanning Castle Eden Burn where it emerges from a culvert beneath a huge embankment carrying the busy A19.

Turn right and follow a broad path downstream. Cross two footbridges close together, but don't cross any more. Keep to the northern side of the river, to follow the path as it climbs back up to Gunners Pool Bridge. Don't cross the bridge, but stay on the northern side and follow a broad path across the wooded slopes. Don't be tempted down on any lesser paths, but aim to stay high. Eventually, a much broader track is reached which runs down from Oakerside Dene Lodge.

A detour up to the **lodge** is recommended, as it houses a visitor centre dedicated to Castle Eden Dene. Here there is the opportunity to obtain detailed information about the geology and natural history of the area, or have a chat with rangers, who sometimes lead guided walks. There is also a café on site, tel 0191 5860004.

Castle Eden dates from the mid-18th century

Ten towering brick arches carry the coastal railway line across the lower part of Castle Eden Dene

The Dene Mouth was originally salt marsh, but was covered in coal-spoil washed from nearby collieries.

Follow the broad track down towards Castle Bridge. Don't cross the bridge, but turn left along another prominent track. The track runs close to Castle Eden Burn and passes below a crumbling cliff of magnesian limestone. Cross over a bridge and continue downstream, passing two enormous limestone boulders. The next bridge should be recognised as the Garden of Eden Bridge, which was crossed earlier in the walk. Cross it again and walk along the broad track to return to the A1086.

At this point, either return to Horden, or consider extending the walk down to the Dene Mouth. To visit the Dene Mouth, cross the busy road to find a gateway on the far side. Walk down a broad tarmac path to a sewage works under the highest of the 10 towering brick arches of a railway viaduct. Continue along a clear path to reach the coast at the **Dene Mouth**, or vary the approach by walking through a wildflower meadow off to the right. ◄

The Durham coast path could be followed north or south, but to return to Horden, simply retrace your steps to the main road.

WALK 9
Wingate and Station Town

Start/Finish	Railway Crossings, Wingate – GR 400 370
Distance	9km (5½ miles)
Terrain	Easy low-level field paths and tracks
Maps	OS Landranger 93; Explorers 305 and 306
Refreshments	Pubs at Wingate or off-route at Trimdon Colliery
Transport	Regular daily buses serve Wingate, Station Town and Trimdon Colliery from Durham and Hartlepool

Three railway lines once converged to form a large triangular junction in the countryside near Wingate and Station Town. This short walk crosses, or even follows, the old trackbeds. Wingate has existed for centuries, while Station Town was built as a colliery village in the 19th century. A selection of footpaths around the villages is combined with short walks along the old trackbeds. Those who are keen on railway walks could explore further afield, as the old lines have found a new use as walking, cycling and horse-riding routes.

The three railways that once converged near Wingate and Station Town can all be followed away from the area by dedicated railway ramblers. The **Hart to Haswell Way** is based on a railway that operated from 1835 until 1980. The **Castle Eden Walkway** can be followed southwards to Stockton-on-Tees or northwards to Sunderland. The other railway ran west and linked with lines at Ferryhill. Coal was the primary commodity carried on all the lines.

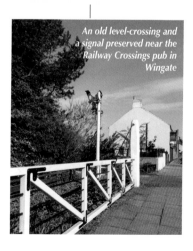
An old level-crossing and a signal preserved near the Railway Crossings pub in Wingate

The area of **Wingate** around the Railway Crossings pub and Bobby G's restaurant preserves an old level-crossing. Follow the B1280 gently up through the village, noting how it bends to the right as it passes a church. The moment the road veers left, turn right along Moor Lane, which quickly becomes a track. Follow the track straight ahead, keeping left of the small fishing lake to reach a broad railway trackbed.

Turn right, but don't follow the trackbed. Instead, follow a narrow path gently uphill and continue past a concrete marker between stone blocks and walk through a field. This area lies in the centre of an enormous triangular railway junction. Pass beneath a pylon line before landing on another old railway trackbed.

Turn right to follow the trackbed, which is the Hart to Haswell Way. Walk as far as a concrete tunnel where the busy A19 crosses. Don't go through the tunnel, but turn right up a bank and descend into a small woodland beyond. The path might be overgrown but look out for a footbridge spanning a stream.

Climb uphill from the river, out of the woods, and turn right along the edge of a field. Look ahead for stiles and a small footbridge, which show the way towards Carrs Pond. While passing this pond, bear slightly left to reach a farm access road, and follow it straight up to a road, where there is a view of the distant Cleveland Hills.

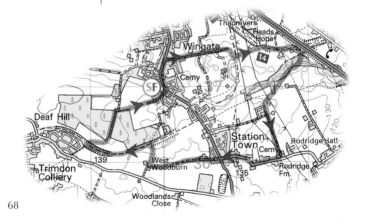

Turn right along the road, passing a cemetery on the way down to **Station Town**. Walk straight through a crossroads, and the road quickly becomes a farm road, then a grassy path running alongside fields. Walk to the next farm, which is **West Woodburn**. Turn right to walk downhill, but stay in the fields, not on the farm access road. The waymarked path is overgrown, forcing walkers onto the edge of an adjacent field. Cross a footbridge over a small stream and climb up onto another old railway trackbed, now used as a walking route. Turn left to follow this until you are close to houses at Trimdon Colliery.

At this point, turn sharp right and climb up the banking to follow an obvious tarmac path, then cross a field. Continue straight through Dead Horse Wood to reach a junction of paths at the far side. Timber extraction has resulted in the track becoming very muddy and rutted at the edge of the wood, but look to the right to spot a clear tarmac path flanked by fences. Follow this through the woods back to Wingate and the Railway Crossings pub.

Wingate Grange Colliery provided employment for miners for 125 years. An explosion at the pit killed 26 miners and 86 pit ponies. The ponies were all buried together in the area now known as **Dead Horse Wood**.

A fishing lake is passed soon after following Moor Lane out of Wingate

WALK 10
Cassop and Quarrington

Start/Finish	Cassop post office – GR 344 383
Distance	8km (5 miles)
Terrain	Easy low-level field paths, tracks and roads
Maps	OS Landranger 93; Explorer 305
Refreshments	Pub and restaurant at Cassop and a pub off-route at Quarrington Hill
Transport	Regular daily buses serve Cassop and Quarrington Hill from Durham and Sedgefield

The area around Cassop and Quarrington has been quarried, mined and crisscrossed by mineral railways. Quarrying still takes place, but today the aspect is pastoral and agricultural. Cassop, Old Cassop, Old Quarrington and Quarrington Hill are settlements occupying elevated ground overlooking the Durham countryside. Who would believe that such enterprises as Cassop Vale Colliery or Crowtrees Colliery once blighted the scene? The vales are now filled with flowery grassland and thorny thickets, and managed as nature reserves. The area is noted for the northern brown argus – a butterfly found only in eastern Durham, where it feeds on the common rock-rose, which in turn flourishes on the thin soils covering the magnesian limestone.

Start at the post office in **Cassop**. Across the road a concrete track runs down to a sewage works in Cassop Vale. However, follow a path to the right, straight across the vale, crossing a footbridge near the pond known as the Bogs. The path threads its way between hawthorn bushes and follows the course of an old mineral line.

Cassop Vale Colliery had its own little settlement, called Cassop-down-the-Hill. The pond known as the Bogs was a product of mining subsidence. Quite apart from the havoc wreaked by mining, German aircraft once dropped bombs on the vale while being pursued by Spitfires. The disturbed ground left by mining suited many rare plants, and Cassop Vale became an 'unoffical' nature reserve quite by chance. It has since been designated a national nature reserve. The rich magnesian limestone soil suits orchids, bird's-eye primrose, blue moor grass, wild thyme and cowslips. Birds devour insects over the pond and pluck fruit from the hawthorns in the appropriate seasons.

Watch out for a track climbing steeply uphill to the right. The gradient eases and the track crosses a broad rise flanked by fields. Turn left through a farmyard, and left again along a quiet road through the lovely little hamlet of **Old Cassop**. ▶ Follow the road downhill until it levels out after crossing Chapman Beck. A footpath sign appears on the right.

There are fine views towards Durham city and the North Pennines.

Cross a stile and turn immediately left to walk roughly parallel to the road along the full length of a narrow field. Later, cross over the road using stiles and follow the path across another field to the main A688 road. This path is a continuation of the old mineral line followed through Cassop Vale earlier.

Cross over the main road and turn left to follow a tarmac path parallel to it. Watch carefully across the road to spot a small gate and a footpath signpost. Cross the road to go through this gate, then turn right and follow a track that passes beneath a bridge near **Heugh Hall Farm**. Follow a track onwards, climbing

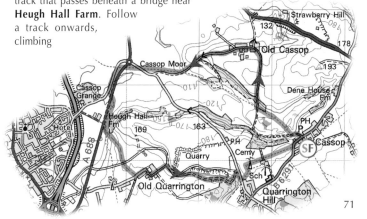

71

uphill. Cross a quarry access road and continue through fields to a road near Heugh Hall Row.

Turn left along the road, which only serves **Old Quarrington**. Follow a broad and obvious track onwards, which leads uphill and suddenly turns right. Continue alongside a quarry, rising, falling and rising again, eventually reaching a road beside a **cemetery**.

> **St Paul's Church** was built in 1868 and was a landmark before it was demolished in 1993. The old churchyard is managed as if it was a hay meadow, partly to control hawthorn scrub, but also to allow seeds to fall and maintain the mix of species. Seed-rich mowings are taken away from the cemetery to help improve other sites around County Durham. A dozen rare plants and scores of rare insects have

A grassy track rises away from Heugh Hall Farm

The path passes a quarry on its way up to Quarrington Hill

been noted in the churchyard. The North Pennines and Cleveland Hills are in view.

Turn right to follow the road towards the village of **Quarrington Hill**, overlooking the vale where Crowtrees Colliery operated from 1825 until 1897. ▶ Turn left on reaching the first houses to follow a track up to a prominent mast on Beacon Hill. Squeeze past the mast to reach a junction of paths. Turn right to follow a track, keeping to the left of a farm. A field path continues straight back to the village of Cassop. Turn left along the road to finish back at the post office.

A detour into the village reveals the Half Moon pub.

73

WALK 11
Sedgefield and Hardwick Hall

Start/Finish	Sedgefield Parish Church – GR 356 288
Distance	8.5km (5¼ miles) or 12.5km (7¾ miles)
Terrain	Easy low-level field paths and tracks
Maps	OS Landranger 93; Explorer 305
Refreshments	Plenty of choice around Sedgefield
Transport	Regular daily buses serve Sedgefield from Durham, Newcastle, Darlington, Bishop Auckland, Sunderland and Hartlepool

Two routes are offered from Sedgefield. One heads southwards from the village, crossing rolling fields and almost reaching the farmstead of Shotton; the other route is simply a short stroll westwards to visit Hardwick Country Park. The medieval Manor of Hardwick was graced with Hardwick Hall in the 1750s, and the grounds were extensively landscaped. After falling into disrepair, the grounds have been restored, and there is a splendid educational resource with a visitor centre. Hardwick Hall is now a hotel.

The main roads crossing at **Sedgefield** are based on old Roman roads, and a settlement grew up there. Bishop Cutheard bought the village of Ceddesfield for the church in 915, and it belonged to the Bishops of Durham until 1836. A market charter was granted in 1312 and there is a full range of facilities. A curious Shrove Tuesday ball game dates from the 13th century, and was originally played between farmers and tradesmen. There is a long tradition of horseracing, and a race course is located to the south of the village. The parish church dominates the spacious central green, and has done for seven centuries, though most buildings seen around the village date from the late 17th century. The central parts form a conservation area that is well worth exploring.

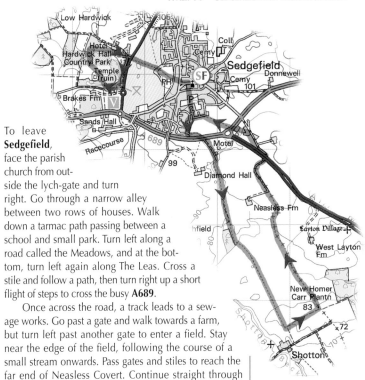

To leave **Sedgefield**, face the parish church from outside the lych-gate and turn right. Go through a narrow alley between two rows of houses. Walk down a tarmac path passing between a school and small park. Turn left along a road called the Meadows, and at the bottom, turn left again along The Leas. Cross a stile and follow a path, then turn right up a short flight of steps to cross the busy **A689**.

Once across the road, a track leads to a sewage works. Go past a gate and walk towards a farm, but turn left past another gate to enter a field. Stay near the edge of the field, following the course of a small stream onwards. Pass gates and stiles to reach the far end of Neasless Covert. Continue straight through fields, rising gently and passing a solitary tree. Eventually, farm buildings are seen ahead at **Shotton**.

Turn left to cross a stile before reaching Shotton, crossing fields with a view of the North York Moors beyond smoky Teesside. Turn left again at a gate to walk along Yarm Lane. This rather rutted old byway runs past large fields, and is closed to all users, apart from walkers, while awaiting repairs. Turn right along a wooded track, which becomes a farm access road leading to the busy A177.

Cross the road and follow a stretch of older road that has now been bypassed. Turn left through a farmyard and pass the Travelodge motel. Cross over the busy A689 turn

75

left as signposted. Follow a tarmac path beside a road through the new housing development of St Edmund's Manor. Continue into the old part of Sedgefield to return to the church.

The grassy Yarm Lane is followed from Shotton to Sedgefield

This walk can also be extended to Hardwick Hall Country Park. Leave Sedgefield by walking through a prominent archway at the Hardwick Arms. Continue along a field path away from the village, bearing left at a kissing gate. Cross the busy A177 and go through the Hardwick Hall Hotel gateway. Turn left to follow a road past small car parks and a folly to reach the information centre for **Hardwick Hall Country Park**. A recommended tour of the site would be a clockwise circuit through the wooded areas beside the lakes. A slightly wider circuit just inside the perimeter of the park tends to be used by cyclists. Afterwards, simply retrace steps back across the fields to Sedgefield.

Hardwick Hall dates from the 1750s and is now a hotel, with the former grounds now a country park. An ornamental lake on the site was overwhelmed by vegetation, and the Serpentine Lake is a remnant of it, while the Fen Carr features the vegetation that largely engulfed it. Hardwick Country Park is a splendid educational resource with a visitor centre. There are also play areas for children with energy to burn. If specific information is needed, look out for the ranger, or tel 03000 262899.

A quaint part of Sedgefield, seen from one of its many central greens

WALK 12

Middleton One Row and Girsby

Start/Finish	Middleton One Row – GR 352 123
Distance	14km (9 miles)
Terrain	Easy low-level riverside and field paths, with tracks and roads
Maps	OS Landranger 93; Explorer 304
Refreshments	Pub at Middleton One Row
Transport	Buses serve Middleton One Row from Darlington and Teesside International Airport

In this relatively flat area, entrenched meanders on the River Tees are so convoluted that within a short distance the river flows north, south, east and west. The Romans built a bridge across the Tees near Middleton One Row. Sulphurous spa waters were discovered by accident in 1789, and by 1842 a bath house was constructed at Dinsdale Park. This walk leads upstream from Middleton One Row, following the Tees to a bridge at Dinsdale, crossing into Yorkshire. The walk continues to Girsby, where another bridge crosses back into County Durham. The entire circuit is marked as part of the Teesdale Way, and from the higher parts there are views of the North York Moors.

Middleton One Row stands on top of a steep grassy bank above the entrenched River Tees

A short stretch of road is encountered beside the River Tees near the start of this walk. Pounteys Lane is named after '**Pons Tesie**', a Roman bridge that once spanned the River Tees, but of which no trace remains. Further up the lane is an earthwork, marked on maps as a 'motte'. It might have been associated with the defence of the old bridge, or it might have been established some time before or after the Roman occupation of the area.

Middleton One Row spreads along the top of a grassy, wooded bank above a broad meander of the River Tees. A path signposted as the Teesdale Way descends and enters woodland. Follow the wooded riverside path faithfully upstream, continuing along a road to a house, then passing in front of it. Woods give way to fields on the way to a minor road at St John's Church. Turn left to cross a narrow bridge over the River Tees, where the road climbs uphill into Yorkshire.

Continue past **Dinsdale Hall**, and the road becomes a lovely tree-lined avenue with views away to the North York Moors. Watch for a turning on the right signposted as the Teesdale Way and follow a farm access road. Watch for waymarks as the footpath continues through a series of gates and crosses several fields.

Keep just below restored **Hill House** farm, but go between buildings at **White House**. Eventually, the largely rebuilt hamlet of **Girsby** is reached, where a right turn passes an old chapel. Descend steeply using an old track, and pass back into County Durham using the Bridle Bridge over the River Tees. ▶

Walk up a track to reach a road at White Houses, then turn right to walk along the road, which has good grass verges. After passing fields to reach **Liberty Lodge**, watch for another Teesdale Way signpost, revealing a path alongside a field to the right of the road. Follow a woodland edge, and continue straight along this line to proceed

A stone records that the bridge was erected by Theophania Blackett in 1870.

79

The River Tees as seen from the Bridle Bridge near Girsby

through more fields to reach another minor road. Turn right and walk down the road, then turn left at a footpath sign.

A good track leads past a **golf course**, and is followed until a right turn is made along an access road. This leads through the grounds of **Dinsdale Park**, then continues downhill to reach a path on the banks of the River Tees. Turn left along the riverside path, which is the one that was used at the start of the day. Follow it up from the wooded riverside to Middleton One Row at the top of the grassy bank.

Miners exploring for coal in 1789 released a spring of smelly, sulphurous water from the rock. This was reckoned to be a cure for all sorts of ailments and was used locally. With the increasing popularity of spas in other parts of the country, a decision was later made to develop **Dinsdale Spa**. A specially constructed bath house was in place in 1842, then a large hotel was built at Dinsdale Park to accommodate all the visitors who were 'taking the waters'. Dinsdale Station was constructed on the nearby railway to offer an alternative to horse-drawn transport. The station survives and the former hotel is now a housing complex.

WALK 13
Low and High Coniscliffe

Start/Finish	Broken Scar picnic area – GR 258 139
Distance	12km (7½ miles)
Terrain	Easy low-level riverside and field paths, with some farm tracks
Maps	OS Landranger 93; Explorer 304
Refreshments	Pub near Low Coniscliffe
Transport	Regular daily buses serve Broken Scar, Low and High Coniscliffe from Darlington and Barnard Castle

Low Coniscliffe and High Coniscliffe can be linked by a stretch of the Teesdale Way that is faithful to the course of the river. After looping round broad meanders and finding an unexpected wilderness area, walkers can return from High Coniscliffe to Low Coniscliffe through the rolling fields around Coniscliffe Grange. High Coniscliffe features a fine church dedicated to St Edwin, which stands behind a crenellated wall perched above the River Tees. This walk could be started at either Low or High Coniscliffe, but it is worth including the Broken Scar picnic area on the outskirts of Darlington.

Start at the Broken Scar picnic area and follow the busy A67 away from the outskirts of Darlington. Pass a waterworks and cross **Baydale Beck** near the Baydale Beck Inn. A footpath on the left leads straight across fields to **Low Coniscliffe**. Follow a minor road left on entering the village, then turn left again onto another footpath. Follow a wooded stretch of the Teesdale Way running upstream from Low Coniscliffe to High Coniscliffe. The riverbank features a broad, wooded path which passes beneath the A1(M).

Continue upstream to reach a tight bend in the course of the river, where swirling currents have cut into the opposite bank and deposited masses of sand and gravel on our side of the river. The gravel spit is clothed in thickets of willow, elder, hazel and hawthorn, though it can be avoided by short-cutting through fields. Head further upstream, passing from fields into another wooded area after crossing **Ulnaby Beck**. The riverside path continues to High Coniscliffe, where a short climb leads to the left of St Edwin's Church.

The place name **Coniscliffe** occurs three times on this short circular walk – Low Coniscliffe, High Coniscliffe and Coniscliffe Grange. It is derived from the Saxon 'Ciningscliffe', which means 'king's cliff'. The parish church at High Coniscliffe stands on top of a low cliff above the River Tees, and is dedicated to St Edwin, King of Northumbria. There is still a little Saxon stonework to be found in the building, but much of the early work dates from the 13th century. This is apparently the only church in the country dedicated to St Edwin.

Turn right along the main road in **High Coniscliffe**, and left after passing a former pub called the Spotted Dog. A short access road leads to a former mill. Pass through a gate to the right of the old mill, cross a footbridge and follow a grassy path through woodland. Go through a gateway into a field and immediately turn right as marked by a yellow arrow. Follow a path along the grassy

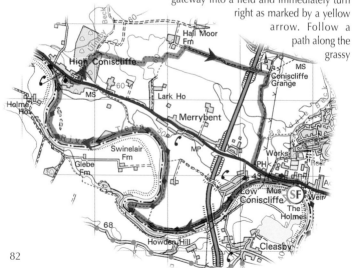

A path alongside the River Tees near High Conscliffe

edge of a field – this is well supplied with stiles, so keep looking ahead to spot each one in turn.

When a track is reached, turn left and walk towards farm buildings at **Hall Moor**. Don't go through the farm-yard, but cut off to the right and bypass the farm using a field path. Waymark arrows indicate the way through fields until another grassy track is reached. Turn right along this track and follow it across a bridge spanning the busy A1(M).

A footpath heads straight onwards beside a field, so there is no need to go between the buildings at **Conscliffe Grange**. Turn right along another track, and follow this gently downhill through fields until the A67 is reached near Low Conscliffe. Turn left along the main road, passing the Baydale Beck Inn and the waterworks on the way back to the Broken Scar picnic area.

The **Tees Cottage Pumping Station** is a working museum operated by enthusiasts, and is devoted to the mechanics of water supply. Several pumping engines can be seen, as well as a blacksmith's shop. There is also a tearoom offering snacks on site. Opening times are limited to about five weekends a year www.teescottage.co.uk.

WALK 14
Gainford and Piercebridge

Start/Finish	Gainford Cross – GR 170 168
Distance	19.5km (12 miles)
Terrain	Easy low-level riverside and field paths, with some farm tracks
Maps	OS Landrangers 92 and 93; Explorer 304
Refreshments	Pubs at Gainford, Piercebridge and Winston
Transport	Regular daily buses serve Winston, Gainford and Piercebridge from Darlington and Barnard Castle

A succession of lovely, interesting villages can be found alongside the River Tees, and most of them are linked by the Teesdale Way. This route takes in Winston, Gainford and Piercebridge, which are all long-established villages. Piercebridge features the remains of a Roman fort and a nearby Roman bridge, strategically sited on Dere Street, which was one of the most important Roman roads in northern England. This walk uses both sides of the River Tees, but while the north bank is followed faithfully, paths and tracks to the south often run far from the riverside.

Start at Gainford Cross on the spacious green in the middle of **Gainford**. Walk out of the village as if following the main road in the direction of Darlington, passing the Gainford Surgery. The roadside path expires, but a signpost on the right reveals a kissing gate and a field path flanked by fences. Follow this and it drifts towards the **River Tees**, with prominent Snow Hall in view. Simply follow the riverside path, marked as the Teesdale Way, to the village of **Piercebridge**, where there are pubs, and an award-winning organic farm shop and café.

Roman remains abound around **Piercebridge**. Head into the village and watch for a sign pointing off the village green to find the excavated remains of a Roman fort, built around AD300.

Noticeboards explain the full extent of the fort, most of which remains buried beneath the village. To visit the Roman bridge, head downstream from the George Hotel as signposted. Massive stone blocks remain in situ on what was the southern bank of the Tees, though the river has shifted northwards since the bridge was built. Stone piers are thought to have supported timber spans. The Roman road Dere Street crossed the bridge on its way from York, through Durham, to Scotland.

Leave Piercebridge by crossing a bridge over the River Tees. A path climbs straight uphill through woodland, continuing through fields where the Cliffe Cricket Club pavilion lies well to the right. Turn right along an iron-railed estate road and follow it straight past a turning for **Cliffe Hall**. Watch for a stile on the left, cross it, and follow a path alongside a field. Keep an eye on prominent **Allan's Grange** farm, and turn right along a grassy track towards it.

Pass in front of the farm, along another grassy track, then turn left to cross a stile. Pick up another track and turn right to follow it away from the farm, then follow

Looking upstream along the River Tees from Piercebridge

more grassy tracks alongside fields. Keep to the right of **Burnthouse Plantation** to reach a minor road. Turn right along it, then left along a farm track at **Low Field**. Follow the track right and left to pass farmhouses, then continue onwards to reach **Chapel House**.

Keep left of all buildings to go through a gate. Walk straight ahead alongside a field, then keep to the same direction alongside hedges to pass from field to field. Eventually, the route swings north and lands on a tarmac farm road. Turn left to follow the road, then turn right at a junction. Turn left along another road that later drops down past the ruins of 12th-century **St Lawrence's Chapel**. Walk past houses in the farming hamlet of Barforth, watching for a public bridleway arrow on a small gate on the left.

The way ahead is vague, so walk through gates and always keep a hedgerow to your left. Later, a track runs beside the River Tees, passing a farm at **Hedgeholme**, followed by a couple of houses. Watch for a gate on the right that allows further access to the riverside, and walk to Winston Bridge. Cross the bridge and turn right to pick

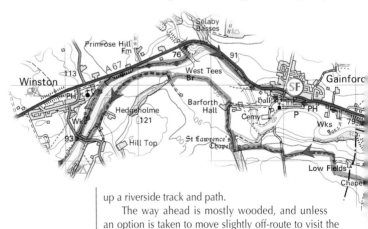

up a riverside track and path.

The way ahead is mostly wooded, and unless an option is taken to move slightly off-route to visit the village of **Winston** and its pub, the path being followed climbs to a lay-by, then runs downstream to reach an old railway bridge. Climb steps onto the old railway embankment and turn left to reach the busy **A67**.

Turn right to follow the road, which soon climbs uphill. Turn right down a path signposted for Gainford Spa to reach a restored and overwhelmingly sulphurous spring. Follow a riverside path downstream towards Gainford, though it is necessary to enter the village using the main road, catching a glimpse of the restored Gainford Hall. However, a right turn down Low Road leads back to the broad and peaceful central green and Gainford Cross.

Gainford and Barforth lie either side of the River Tees at a point where it could be forded. Apparently both communities vied with each other for control of the ford, and while those on the southern side barred the use of the ford ('bar ford' – Barforth), those on the northern side gained control of it ('gain ford' – Gainford). A monastery was built here in the 9th century, on a site now occupied by the 13th-century parish church. Stout Gainford Hall can be glimpsed at the western end of the village, while towards the eastern end, former Gainford Academy once counted the actor Stan Laurel among its students, when he travelled here from his home in Bishop Auckland. (Although Stan Laurel was born in Ulverston, he spent his formative years at Bishop Auckland.)

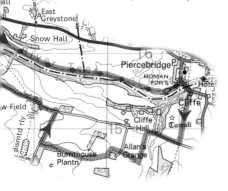

WALK 15
Cockfield Fell and Butterknowle

Start/Finish	St Mary's Church, Cockfield – GR 129 243
Distance	11km (7 miles)
Terrain	Gentle hill-walking using fairly clear paths and tracks
Maps	OS Landranger 92; Explorer 305
Refreshments	A couple of pubs at Cockfield and Butterknowle
Transport	Regular daily buses serve Cockfield from Bishop Auckland and Barnard Castle. Fewer buses serve Butterknowle and Burnt Houses.

Cockfield and Butterknowle are perched on high ground on opposite sides of the River Gaunless. Most of the surrounding land is enclosed and cultivated, but the northern slope of Cockfield Fell remains as rough pasture, featuring open access as well as being a scheduled ancient monument. This walk wanders round the fell before crossing the River Gaunless to climb to Butterknowle. After recrossing the Gaunless, the route follows the boundary wall of Raby Park before returning to Cockfield. There are plenty of reminders of former industry, and Cockfield claims to have had the earliest recorded colliery, dating from 1365, although it is certain that people have used coal for much longer.

St Mary's Church is at the bottom end of **Cockfield** village. A footpath sign opposite the church points along a road passing a cemetery. The road traverses the open slopes of **Cockfield Fell** and crosses the line of an old whinstone quarry. Follow the road up past Fell Houses, then continue down towards the River Gaunless. Turn left before reaching the river and climb up to an old railway viaduct buttress.

Turn left to walk along the old railway trackbed, until passing beneath a **pylon line**. At this point, turn right and follow a path beside a prominent trench, passing some disturbed ground that is an ancient enclosure. Walk down to the River Gaunless, turn left and walk upstream, though the riverside path soon expires. Climb high above

the riverbank and descend again later to pick up and follow a track that eventually passes a sewage works.

Cross an access track and then a stone bridge, and
then squeeze between the gardens of two houses to reach
a road. Go straight ahead along the road, then turn right
towards the village of Butterknowle.

*Pigeon lofts and
sheds erected by
Cockfield residents
on the higher parts
of Cockfield Fell*

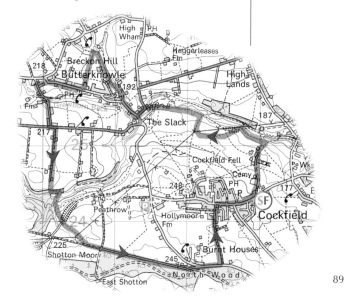

As the road bends left on entering the lower part of Butterknowle, known as **the Slack**, head off to the right along a track. Follow a muddy path upstream alongside Crow Howle Beck, avoiding a footbridge signposted 'Pedestrians Only'. Progress upstream and look out for igloo-like coke ovens. The interior brickwork of the coke ovens has fused under extremely high temperatures. Cross a footbridge on the left then turn right to walk uphill. Turn left through gates a little later to follow a path across fields to **Butterknowle**. A road is reached beside The Royal Oak pub. Turn right to walk to the top end of the village.

Look out for a path on the left on reaching the end of the village. This merely short-cuts through a farm and avoids a nearby road junction. Turn left down a road, crossing **Grewburn Beck** near a picnic area. The Quarry Pit was sunk nearby and closed in 1942. Follow the road uphill and turn left at the top, then turn right along a farm

A flowery field is passed through on the way back into Butterknowle

access road, signposted as a public footpath, and not the concrete road serving a fuel depot.

Keep to the right of the last building on this track and continue along a field path. Turn left along the top edge of a wooded slope. Later, turn sharp right down a track to reach a gate, then ford the River Gaunless. In wet weather, this will mean wet feet, but the walk is coming to a close.

Walk uphill from the ford and keep close to a wall and fence that lead to an old railway bridge. Cross over the bridge and walk straight onwards through fields to join a narrow road. Bear left to follow this road, which is also accompanied by the tall boundary wall of Raby Park. The road leads to **Burnt Houses**.

Turn right along a minor road at Burnt Houses, then left at a gate along a clear grassy track. This track runs straight back towards Cockfield, reaching the middle of the village by way of Coronation Terrace. Simply turn right and head downhill to bring the walk to an end.

Cockfield Fell has never been fully enclosed, although it has been settled, quarried, mined and crossed by a railway line. Cockfield people graze horses, sheep and cattle on the fell, and have erected pigeon lofts. A body known as the Field Reeves regulates the use of the fell. An old whinstone quarry was cut into a dolerite dyke that extends much further across country. Part of the quarry was used as an infill site, and when it was closed the original contours of the fell were restored. The old railway line crossing Cockfield Fell was part of the South Durham and Lancashire Union Railway, dating from 1862. It lasted for a century and had a number of lofty viaducts – nearly all of which have been demolished. Less obvious on the rumpled ground of the fell are a series of much older earthworks, which are thought to be both Romano–British and pre-Roman settlements. Cockfield Fell is said to be the largest scheduled ancient monument in England.

WALK 16
Woodland and Copley

Start/Finish	Woodland – GR 075 265
Distance	8.5km (5 miles)
Terrain	Easy low-level field paths and tracks, with some slopes
Maps	OS Landranger 92; Explorer OL31
Refreshments	Pub at Woodland
Transport	Weekday buses serve Woodland from Cockfield, Barnard Castle and Bishop Auckland

Woodland and Copley are at the top of the Gaunless Valley, in an area where several small-scale coalmines once operated, even into the 20th century. A short walk through the area reveals the remains of former industry, with pit spoils, shafts, old tramways, and a landmark chimney once linked with a smelt mill at an old lead mine.

Start in **Woodland** at the Edge Hotel and walk down the road signposted for Bishop Auckland. Views stretch to the distant North York Moors, to the left, and the North Pennines, to the right. At the bottom of the road, turn left along the farm access road for **Lunton Hill**. Go through the farmyard and follow the track onwards through fields, then walk downhill by road past **Lynesack Church**. Turn right at the bottom then, when the road turns left, keep straight ahead instead.

Look for a narrow path enclosed by bushes, which continues through fields to a farmhouse lying upstream beside **Howle Beck**. Turn left to cross the beck, and also cross two access tracks close together while walking a short way uphill. A footpath marker reveals a way round the right-hand side of a house. Cross fields, looking ahead for a gate and stile, and especially watching for a narrow path running between gardens leading to the road in the village of **Copley**.

Cross the road, turning right and immediately left to walk past Chapel Terrace. Head down through fields to Low Trough Farm, and keep left of it to find a footpath down through fields. This

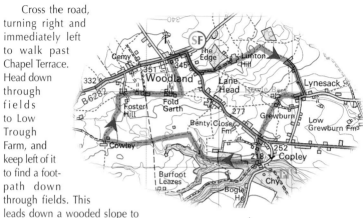

leads down a wooded slope to land on a track just above a house. This was the Manager's House for a former lead-smelting mill. ▶

If not visiting the chimney, simply turn right to follow the path through Cowclose Plantation. Exit into a field to follow a grassy embankment. Turn right at gate and walk straight onwards, then turn left at gate into Cowclose Wood. Head up from the wood into fields, where the path is vague, but climb and drift to the left.

Pick up a grassy track running through gates, then fork left, away from a colliery track and the old Woodland Tramway, to cross a footbridge and follow a grassy track. Study a notice about the Cowley Colliery, then walk past the ruins of **Cowley Farm**.

Go through a gateway and turn right, watching for stiles on the way through fields, and cross over two runnels of water on the way up to a farm. The path runs between fences as you turn right to pass the farm, then keep watching for stiles while walking from one farm to another in a straight line.

After passing the last farm, which is **Fold Garth**, cross a field, but don't cross a stile ahead. Instead, turn left to climb back to Woodland, reaching a road at corrugated-iron church. Turn right along a road to finish at the Edge Hotel.

The prominent chimney in view carried poisonous fumes from the site, and it can be visited by making a short detour off-route from a car park just across the river.

An old lead smelting mill chimney can be visited near Copley

WALK 17
Staindrop and Cleatlam

Start/Finish	South Green, Staindrop – GR 127 206
Distance	9km (5½ miles)
Terrain	Easy low-level field paths, but vague in places, with some slopes
Maps	OS Landranger 92; Explorers 304 and 305
Refreshments	Pubs in Staindrop
Transport	Regular daily buses serve Staindrop from Bishop Auckland and Barnard Castle

Staindrop is a long and straggly village featuring several splendid buildings and a series of interconnected greens. Its history is very much bound up with that of Raby Castle, the seat of Lord Barnard. This walk offers an opportunity to explore the village of Staindrop, and enjoy the gentle agricultural countryside all around it. The circuit closes with a walk alongside the tall boundary wall of Raby Park. If Raby Castle is open to visitors, then a tour might be included before or after the walk. Distant views, particularly from around Cleatlam, extend across County Durham from the plains to the North Pennines.

Starting from the South Green in **Staindrop**, locate the Scarth Memorial Hall, where Stangarth Lane is signposted as a public footpath. Walk along the narrow road between the buildings, then later turn right along a short track and cross a stile into a field. Head diagonally left across the field, and look ahead to spot the necessary stiles until a minor road is reached. Turn left to cross a nearby bridge over **Sudburn Beck**, and walk a little further uphill.

Look for a footpath sign on the right that shows the way into a field. Walk back downhill and keep to the edge of the field, first using the course of Sudburn Beck as a guide. Later, turn left and walk uphill at a gentle gradient through the fields to reach another minor road just outside **Cleatlam**. Turn right and follow the road all the way through this pleasant little farming village, enjoying distant views across the fields.

After passing the last farm the road begins to level out. Turn right through a gate and then head diagonally to the left across a field. Look ahead to spot a series of stiles in the walls and fences, which will lead gradually downhill. Keep to the right of a farm, heading straight for the busy A688. Cross over the road and follow an obvious, fenced path downhill. There is a short steep drop to a little wooded river, where a footbridge is crossed. Walk straight uphill, and keep to the right of **Snotterton Hall**.

Follow the access road away from the hall, then turn left at a corner where a gateway bears a waymark. Cross a couple of fields, then look for a right turn across a broad dip that allows a direct approach to **Scaife House**. Cross a culverted stream on the way to Scaife House, then walk through the farmyard and leave via the farm access road. Turn right along the **B6279**, then left up the next access road to **West Lodge**.

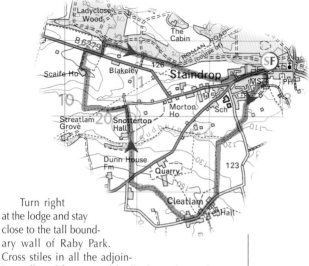

Turn right at the lodge and stay close to the tall boundary wall of Raby Park. Cross stiles in all the adjoining walls and fences, until finally directed away from the wall on the approach to Staindrop. Return to the village using field paths and a narrow alleyway between houses. Continue past all the greens in the village to reach South Green where the walk started.

In 1378, when Lord John Nevill was granted a licence to build Raby Castle, he obtained a market charter for **Staindrop** at the same time. A cattle market flourished until 1858, and in front of Gorst Hall the remains of stone posts and chains can be seen, which used to keep stock away from the houses. Some of the older extant buildings date from the 16th century, but there are also Victorian and Georgian styles. The parish church dates from Saxon times, from around the 8th century, but it has been rebuilt, extended and enlarged many times. The village is a designated conservation area.

The Nevill family lost **Raby Castle** after their part in the Rising of the North in 1569. Sir Henry Vane

*The whitewashed
Snotterton Hall lies
between Cleatlam
and Staindrop*

bought the place and the first Lord Barnard came from the Vane family in 1698.

The Raby Estates are an extensive, but patchwork series of holdings stretching all the way to Upper Teesdale, where property is traditionally whitewashed, with the doorposts and lintels painted black. Raby Castle isn't seen properly from this walk, but is seen briefly from the road linking Staindrop with Bishop Auckland. The park wall surrounding Raby Park and the castle measures about 14km (9 miles) in circumference. The Great Kitchen in the castle was used for six centuries, but the castle itself has been altered and extended. There are collections of art inside, while the grounds have been landscaped and feature fine gardens. There is also a coach house with an assortment of horse-drawn carriages. An extensive deer park is populated by large herds of red and fallow deer in a variety of colours.

The castle and grounds are open to visitors on certain days in the summer, tel 01833 660202, www.raby.co.uk.

WALK 18

Greta Bridge and Brignall Banks

Start/Finish	Greta Bridge – GR 086 133
Distance	11km (7 miles) or 15km (9 miles)
Terrain	A steep-sided gorge with narrow woodland and field paths
Maps	OS Landranger 92; Explorer OL30 or OL31
Refreshments	Pub at Greta Bridge
Transport	Buses serve Greta Bridge from Barnard Castle and Richmond, except Sundays

Before the River Greta reaches its confluence with the mighty River Tees at the Meeting of the Waters, it flows by way of Brignall Banks, through a deep, wooded gorge between Rutherford Bridge and Greta Bridge. Between the bridges the gorge is exceptionally well wooded. Apart from Brignall Mill and the ruins of St Mary's Church, there are no signs of settlement deep in the gorge. The journey through the gorge uses paths on both sides of the river, and is rather like a jungle trek, in contrast to the sheep-cropped pastures at a higher level. Recent signposting indicates the 'Greta Walk' and offers an extension to Bowes.

Start on the same side of Greta Bridge as the Morritt Arms and walk across the graceful span of the bridge. Pass a fine courtyard building, then turn right at a gap between the farm buildings alongside. Go through a gate, out of the farmyard, and walk across a field before following a path gently uphill through a small wood. Turn right along a minor road, then later turn right again round a sharp bend to reach **Wilson House**.

Follow the farm access road from Wilson House to **Crook's House**. Head off to the right before reaching the farm, and follow a rather muddy path towards the edge of a wood. Keep to the edge of the wood until it can be entered at a waymarked gateway. Stay by the inner edge of the wood until the path leads down through the

wood to reach the banks of Gill Beck. Ford the beck using stepping stones (which could be difficult when the water is in spate).

Once across Gill Beck, follow the path uphill and proceed across a steep slope high above the **River Greta**. Part of this path features a safety fence above a steep drop. Later, the path descends and runs upstream, joining a clearer path to reach a footbridge giving access to Brignall Mill. (If this footbridge is crossed, a right turn allows the walk to be shortened, otherwise the route can be extended further upstream to Rutherford Bridge.)

To complete the extra distance, don't cross the footbridge, but follow the clear path up to the edge of the wood. Turn right to walk alongside the wood and watch for a path heading back down to the riverside. Continue upstream, but watch for a path rising gradually up from the woods again, passing through small fields. This path leads to a minor road, which is followed downhill to cross the graceful arch of Rutherford Bridge.

Walk uphill a short way on the road, then turn right as indicated by a footpath sign. The path itself is rather vague, but the idea is to keep to the grassy brow above the wooded gorge. Brignall Mill, which was seen earlier in the walk, will be noticed before its access track is reached, but the route doesn't go down to the building. (Those who took the short-cut, however, will climb up this track.)

Cross the access track and continue alongside a field until a clear path runs down through the woods to reach the riverside. Follow the path through the wooded gorge, and later emerge into fields to reach the ruins and old graveyard of **St Mary's Church**. Climb gradually up from the ruins, following a path just outside the woodland edge. Eventually, this path leads down towards Greta Bridge, where a stone step-stile leads back onto the road near the Morritt Arms.

Greta Bridge and **Brignall Banks** attracted poets, writers and artists in the 19th century. Cotman painted a view of Greta Bridge, while Turner painted the nearby Meeting of the Waters. Dickens visited the Morritt Arms while researching *Nicholas Nickleby*. Sir Walter Scott praised the scenery in the following lines:

> *O Brignall Banks are wild and fair,*
> *And Greta woods are green,*
> *And you may gather garlands there,*
> *Would grace a summer queen.*

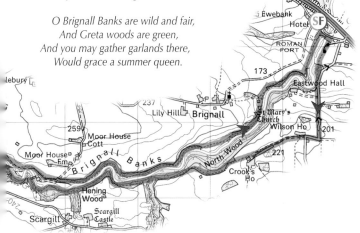

WALK 19
Tan Hill and Sleightholme Moor

Start/Finish	Tan Hill Inn GR 896 067
Distance	14km (9 miles)
Terrain	Rugged, high-level, exposed moorland paths and tracks
Maps	OS Landranger 92; Explorer OL30
Refreshments	Tan Hill Inn
Transport	None

Tan Hill Inn is the highest pub in England, standing at a lonely moorland road junction at 530m (1732ft). It was 'transferred' to County Durham during the local government reorganisation of 1974, and this was a sore point with many locals. The pub was brought back into Yorkshire following a boundary change in April 1991. The Pennine Way passes the door, and the route has in its time been diverted on Sleightholme Moor – its original course became very boggy, so it was transferred across Frumming Beck onto firmer ground. To create a circular walk, an old bridleway across the moors can be linked with a shooting track and a patchy moorland road. For those who wish to stay longer at Tan Hill, accommodation is available.

Walk out of the porch of the **Tan Hill Inn** and turn left to walk up a minor road and cross a cattle-grid. Turn right along a track, but when the track bends to the right, head off to the left instead. A path forges across heathery ground that can be boggy in places. Beware of a **bell pit** just to the left of the path. The route is vague as it crosses the ravine of **Mirk Fell Gill**, but look ahead to spot a low, ruined stone hut, and pass to the right-hand side of it.

The path rises past a capped mine shaft, and it is fairly clear as it crosses **Mirk Fell** at nearly 580m (1900ft). Descend slightly to cross a stream, and be sure to continue onwards to the next stream, which is **William Gill**. While descending towards it, turn left to follow it downstream. A clear track is joined, which crosses and re-crosses the stream using fords and bridges. As the narrow valley begins to widen, the track joins a minor road.

After a rugged moorland walk, an easy track runs down alongside William Gill

Turn left up the minor road and follow it across the moors. Later, turn right along a patchy road signposted for Bowes (marked as the W2W cycle route). Follow this moorland road to a junction with a clear track. Turn left to pass a barrier gate and pass a notice about Bowes Moor. The idea is to follow the Pennine Way back towards Tan Hill Inn. The track crosses a bridge over **Frumming Beck**, then after crossing the bridge, turn left.

Follow a path marked by wooden posts, which keeps well away from the beck, and yet still follows it upstream. Walk mostly on grassy moorland, but beyond some sheepfolds there is more heather cover. After passing a cairn the path runs closer to the beck in its upper reaches. Aim almost directly for the Tan Hill Inn, with the wettest and boggiest stretch coming last. Hit the moorland road just to the left of the buildings, where one stile needs to be crossed before the walk is over.

William Camden mentioned an inn at this remote spot in 1586, but the current structure of the **Tan Hill Inn** dates from the 17th century. The inn stood at a focal point on packhorse ways and caught the passing trade. Bell pits and open mine shafts dot the bleak moors, and coal mining provided a more regular clientele at the Tan Hill Inn. There is good local support for the inn, but it relies heavily on tourist traffic, and Pennine Wayfarers seldom pass it by if the doors are open. Tan Hill Inn has featured on television to promote double-glazing, and in foul weather a blazing fire should be burning, though there may be competition for a fireside seat! A variety of accommodation is available, from bed and breakfast to bunkhouse and camping, tel 01833 533007, www.tanhillinn.com.

The Tan Hill Inn is the highest pub in England at 530m (1732ft)

WALK 20

Bowes and Bowes Moor

Start/Finish	Bowes – GR 995 135
Distance	16km (10 miles)
Terrain	Easy field paths and farm tracks, with exposed moorland paths
Maps	OS Landranger 92; Explorer OL31
Refreshments	Pub at Bowes
Transport	Weekday buses serve Bowes from Barnard Castle

This walk over Bowes Moor makes use of the Pennine Way main route and the alternative Bowes Loop. Bowes is a quiet, pleasant little village with a long history of catering for travellers across Stainmore. It is also the site of Dotheboys Hall, which was made notorious by Charles Dickens. The route leaves Bowes and traces the River Greta upstream to East Mellwaters. By the time God's Bridge is reached, the Pennine Way main route is followed. This crosses desolate Bowes Moor and Deepdale. A short-cut along the moorland crest of Race Yate Rigg enables walkers to transfer onto the course of the Bowes Loop, crossing Deepdale again to return to Bowes.

Travellers have crossed Stainmore for thousands of years, as the broad gap on the Pennine moors allows an obvious east–west link. The Romans regulated traffic by constructing a road equipped with forts, camps and signal stations. The fort at **Bowes** was called Lavatrae, and its square, grassy platform can be discerned, but all its masonry was incorporated into Bowes Castle in 1170. The castle watched over an area that was an unsettled borderland. The Stainmore wastes were bleak, and monastic hospices were established to serve travellers – memory of these places lingers in the place name 'Spital'. A turnpike road was constructed in 1743, and literally paved the way for cross-country coaching, and

Bowes still features coaching architecture, such as
the Ancient Unicorn pub. The South Durham and
Lancashire Union Railway came in 1861, lasting for
a century until closure.

Leave **Bowes** by way of the parish church and walk along
Back Lane to reach **Bowes Castle**. Turn right to walk
beside its perimeter fence and continue through fields to
reach a track. Turn left to follow the track and another
field path to reach a footbridge over the River Greta.

Walk to a farm access road and turn right to follow
it to **West Charity Farm**. Turn right and left to pass the
farm, then cross a footbridge over Sleightholme Beck
(not the bridge over the Greta). Keep right to follow a
path to **East Mellwaters**.

5500 years of farming history
have been excavated around **East
Mellwaters**. Iron Age dwellings were
unearthed beside the farm road, as
well as a rectangular settlement in
a field. A Romano–British house lies
across Sleightholme Beck, while the
modern farmhouse stands on the site of a
medieval dwelling. The farm provides spe-
cialist accommodation for people with dis-
abilities, and a network of easy-use trails has
been established around nearby fields.

Keep right of the buildings to get onto a farm track
running from East Mellwaters to **West Mellwaters**. Go
through a gateway just beyond West Mellwaters and bear
diagonally to the right to cross a field. Once over a low
rise, head straight down to God's Bridge, which is flanked
by old limekilns. Cross over the natural limestone slab that
forms God's Bridge and follow a track uphill from the river.

The busy A66 is at the top of the track, so divert left
and walk beneath the road using an underpass. Turn
right on the other side, then left at **Pasture End** to climb
up a moorland slope. Follow a prominent cairned path

Bowes Castle was built from stone pillaged from a Roman fort

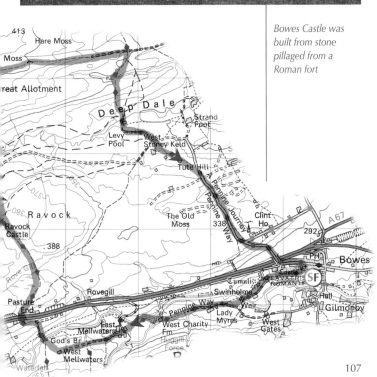

God's Bridge is a remarkable, natural limestone slab with the River Greta flowing beneath it

onwards over a moorland rise, crossing **Rove Gill** and passing the ruined stone hut of **Ravock Castle**, now piled into a cairn. Wander downhill to cross a track beside a hut offering shelter, followed by a footbridge over **Deepdale Beck**. Climb gradually uphill following a wall up the grassy moorland slope.

Just before reaching the top of this slope, at 427m (1402ft) on **Race Yate**, go through a gate on the right. A track made by wheeled vehicles can be followed across the slopes of Race Yate Rigg, and eventually reaches a fence. Turn right, and although it is tempting to walk alongside the fence, drift to the right away from it. Cross little Hazelgill Beck, then use a footbridge to cross Deepdale Beck again at the restored, heather-thatched farm of **Levy Pool**.

Follow the access track up from Levy Pool, joining a tarmac road at **West Stoney Keld**. This leads back to Bowes, but the Pennine Way cuts a bend from it. Walk along the West Stoney Keld access road, and turn left before reaching the farm. Follow a field path back to the road and turn right.

The road leads through an old military site flanked by warning signs. Later, turn right to follow another road downhill and cross over the busy A66. Walk straight into the village of Bowes via Dotheboys Hall, and continue along the main street to the Ancient Unicorn pub.

A fine grassy track is used to ascend Race Yate on the bleak and empty moors of Stainmore

Charles Dickens visited Bowes in 1838 and collected material about the notorious 'Yorkshire Schools', which included **Dotheboys Hall**. He met William Shaw, the headmaster, who was transformed into the character of Wackford Squeers. Some of Dickens' information was gleaned at the bar of the Ancient Unicorn. The furore raised by the publication of Dickens' work resulted in the ultimate closure of the Yorkshire Schools, to the great relief of their ill-treated inmates. The house is not open to the public.

WALK 21
Barnard Castle and the Tees

Start/Finish	Scar Top, Barnard Castle – GR 049 166
Distance	12km (7½ miles)
Terrain	Easy, mostly low-level woodland and riverside paths
Maps	OS Landranger 92; Explorer OL31
Refreshments	Plenty of choice around Barnard Castle
Transport	Regular daily buses serve Barnard Castle from Darlington, Bishop Auckland and Middleton-in-Teesdale. There is also a town bus service.

Riverside paths run along both banks of the River Tees and both sides of Barnard Castle, so it is possible to make an intimate exploration of the river. This walk works its way upstream from Barnard Castle, returning at a higher level to the town. Next, it heads downstream to Abbey Bridge, and offers a chance to visit Egglestone Abbey. Barnard Castle is full of interest and there are many fine buildings in and around the town. The castle dominates the riverside, while Egglestone Abbey and the Bowes Museum occupy commanding ground nearby. As this walk comes in two halves, with Barnard Castle in the middle, different parts of the town can be explored as the walk progresses, though the Bowes Museum needs plenty of time to visit. In due course you'll be referring to the town as 'Barney', as the local folk do.

Start at Scar Top, which is just off Galgate in **Barnard Castle**, near the castle. Bear right to pass a children's play area and follow a tarmac path downhill. Cross a footbridge over Percy Beck (not the large footbridge accompanying the Deepdale Aqueduct, built in 1893). A cobbly path leads upstream beside the **River Tees**, passing through varied and interesting woodlands, with good ground scrub. Walk beneath towering buttresses that once supported a railway viaduct.

The riverside path is known as the Rock Walk, featuring a couple of boulders called the Wishing Stones.

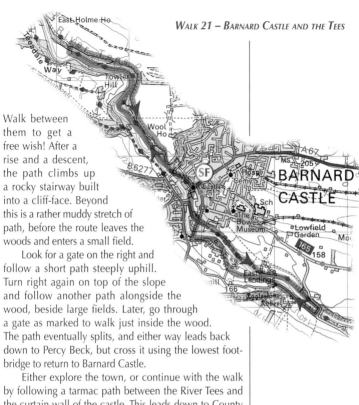

Walk between them to get a free wish! After a rise and a descent, the path climbs up a rocky stairway built into a cliff-face. Beyond this is a rather muddy stretch of path, before the route leaves the woods and enters a small field.

Look for a gate on the right and follow a short path steeply uphill. Turn right again on top of the slope and follow another path alongside the wood, beside large fields. Later, go through a gate as marked to walk just inside the wood. The path eventually splits, and either way leads back down to Percy Beck, but cross it using the lowest footbridge to return to Barnard Castle.

Either explore the town, or continue with the walk by following a tarmac path between the River Tees and the curtain wall of the castle. This leads down to County Bridge. Don't cross the bridge, but walk up the main road as if heading into town. However, when the road turns suddenly left, walk straight ahead along Gray Lane. This runs out into the grassy Demesnes, where a track runs beside the River Tees.

Follow the track downstream, passing an attractive group of houses and later a sewage works. A riverside path continues through fields, into a small wooded area, before rising to Abbey Bridge. Cross this fine arch, then turn right and continue along a minor road. **Egglestone Abbey** is worth a visit, and is reached by turning left up a road. It was a Premonstratensian foundation, whose construction commenced in 1196. After looking round the

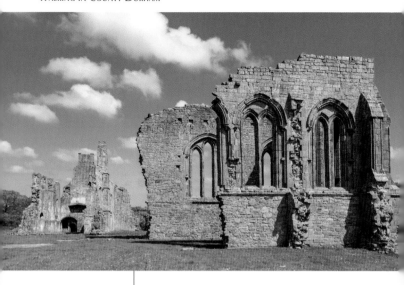

The ruins of Egglestone Abbey can be visited free of charge

ruins, come back down the road and turn left again to pass ancient Bow Bridge.

Look out for a footpath sign on the right, which indicates a field path keeping above the River Tees and passing above a caravan site. Later, drop down through the caravan site and turn left along a riverside path again. Follow this path onto a narrow road, then turn right to cross a footbridge that leads to some old mills across the Tees. Walk straight up Thorngate, and continue up past the octagonal Market Cross to return to Scar Top and Galgate at the top end of Barnard Castle.

The castle from which **Barnard Castle** takes its name was built in the 12th century by Bernard Baliol. Its extensive curtain wall stands high above the River Tees at County Bridge. The bridge is not far from a Roman ford, and has been altered since being built in 1569, successfully replacing other structures. The Market Cross, around which traffic gyrates, is a substantial octagonal building constructed in 1747.

Its colonnaded exterior served as a butter market, while the interior has been used as a town hall, courthouse and jail.

Bowes Museum is a remarkable château, commenced in 1860, and funded from the proceeds of the coal industry by John and Joséphine Bowes. John was a son of the 10th Earl of Strathmore, while Joséphine was a Parisian actress. Between them they amassed an impressive collection of European artworks to fill the museum. Tel 01833 690606, www.thebowesmuseum.org.uk.

The Bowes Museum looks like a French château and is filled with art treasures

WALK 22
Cotherstone and Romaldkirk

Start/Finish	Fox and Hounds, Cotherstone – GR 011 198
Distance	10km (6¼ miles)
Terrain	Easy, but occasionally rugged riverside paths and field paths
Maps	OS Landranger 92; Explorer OL31
Refreshments	Pubs at Cotherstone and Romaldkirk; café off-route at Eggleston Hall
Transport	Regular daily buses serve Cotherstone and Romaldkirk from Barnard Castle and Middleton-in-Teesdale

The long-distance Teesdale Way often uses paths on both sides of the River Tees. Whenever the necessary bridging points allow, circular walks can be enjoyed. The walk round Cotherstone and Romaldkirk is a firm favourite with many walkers. Some paths run close to the River Tees, but there are others climbing high above the river, offering extensive views of the surrounding countryside. Cotherstone and Romaldkirk are attractive, interesting little villages well worth exploring. In between them is the farm of Woden Croft, which was one of the notorious 'Yorkshire Schools' exposed by Charles Dickens. On the opposite side of the River Tees is Percy Mere Rock, a notable viewpoint.

Opposite the Fox and Hounds pub in **Cotherstone**, a narrow road runs steeply downhill and cars can be parked there. Hallgarth Hill, the site of an old castle, overlooks the area. Turn left to cross a footbridge spanning the River Balder, but don't cross a nearby footbridge over the River Tees, which will be crossed at the end of the day's walk. A wooded path leads upstream alongside the River Tees, before drifting uphill and away from the river to reach an old walled garden at **Woden Croft**.

Continue past the farmhouse at Woden Croft, bearing right while passing the buildings, then stay on a track running by a woodland edge. Go through a gate on the

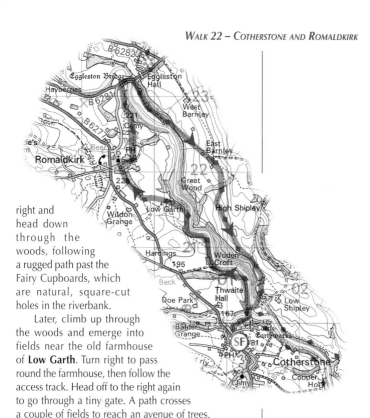

right and head down through the woods, following a rugged path past the Fairy Cupboards, which are natural, square-cut holes in the riverbank.

Later, climb up through the woods and emerge into fields near the old farmhouse of **Low Garth**. Turn right to pass round the farmhouse, then follow the access track. Head off to the right again to go through a tiny gate. A path crosses a couple of fields to reach an avenue of trees. Turn right at that point to pick up a track leading into the village of **Romaldkirk**.

> **Romaldkirk** is one of the most attractive and interesting little villages in Teesdale. There are three greens and two pubs, fine cottages and beautiful gardens. An interesting 12th-century church incorporates a little Saxon stonework, and has a couple of unusual features. One is a blocked-up north doorway, said to have the devil on the other side! Another is the tracery of the east window, which simply doesn't look right. Pevsner declared that it 'looks like a protest against all rules'.

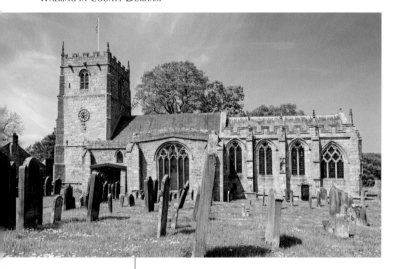

Romaldkirk's parish church has an east window with unusual tracery

An exploration of Romaldkirk is recommended, but to continue the walk, turn right and walk past a green, then turn left to walk down a narrow, hedged path. Cross **Beer Beck** and continue over a rise on the field path, then follow the path down to the B6281 near **Eggleston Bridge**. The bridge was built in the 17th century and is thought to have replaced a 15th-century structure.

Cross over it and turn right along a narrow road (but bear in mind that Eggleston Hall and its café lie nearby). The road leads past a small pavilion, and ends above a tunnel where water from distant Kielder Reservoir occasionally augments the flow of the River Tees.

Just before the tunnel mouth, a stile on the left gives access to a flight of steps climbing up a wooded slope. Emerge into fields on top, then follow a path round the top side of **East Barnley Farm**. The path can be vague afterwards, so look ahead carefully to spot all the necessary waymarks and stiles. Cross Raygill Beck and continue straight across sloping fields to reach the edge of Shipley Wood. Later, cross a wall to stand on the top of Percy Mere Rock.

The last of the Fitzhughs, who were lords of Romaldkirk, went out hunting one day, and was warned to go home by an old woman. Spurning the warning, he continued on his way, and of course should have known better than to hunt anything as unusual as a white deer when night was falling. It was too late to do anything by the time he realised his folly, as he was already plummeting to his death from the precipitous slopes of **Percy Mere Rock**. The rock provides a wonderful vista, stretching towards desolate Stainmore.

Return to the path and turn right to continue the walk. Later, drop down to the right into a wood and pass through a caravan site. Leave the site and continue down to the River Tees. Cross over a long footbridge, then turn left to cross the footbridge over the River Balder, which was used earlier in the day. The nearby road runs straight uphill to Cotherstone, emerging opposite the Fox and Hounds.

The River Tees as seen from Eggleston Bridge below Eggleston Hall

WALK 23

Tees Railway Walk

Start	Middleton-in-Teesdale – GR 947 254
Finish	Fox and Hounds, Cotherstone – GR011198
Distance	11km (7 miles)
Terrain	Easy low-level walking on a railway trackbed
Maps	OS Landranger 92; Explorer OL31
Refreshments	Plenty of choice around Middleton; pubs at Mickleton, Romaldkirk and Cotherstone
Transport	Regular daily bus services link Middleton, Mickleton, Romaldkirk and Cotherstone with Barnard Castle

Middleton-in-Teesdale was once served by a branch line from Barnard Castle. It was built as a private concern and opened in 1868, but was taken over by the North Eastern Railway in 1882. The line enabled quarries near Middleton, biting into the hard Whin Sill, to transport crushed stone out of the dale. Passenger stations were built at Middleton, Romaldkirk and Cotherstone. The Tees Railway Walk links all three sites and can be used by walkers and cyclists. As this is a linear route, walkers can catch a bus back to the start if they wish, although for a longer walk the Teesdale Way offers an alternative return along the riverside.

Middleton-in-Teesdale has 12th-century origins and was close to the hunting and grazing grounds of distant Rievaulx Abbey. The Horsemarket and Market Place point to the settlement's importance in a farming region, and the old market cross and remains of the village stocks survive. Water from Hudeshope Beck powered two corn mills. St Mary's church dates from 1857, but an old arch and detached belfry belong to an earlier church dating from 1557. The churchyard holds the grave of Richard Watson, the celebrated miner-poet of Teesdale. Middleton became an important lead-mining centre and the town was developed considerably by the London Lead Company (see Walk 24).

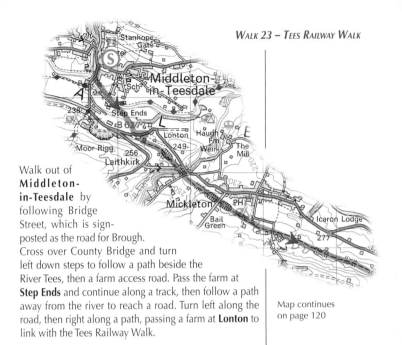

Walk out of **Middleton-in-Teesdale** by following Bridge Street, which is signposted as the road for Brough. Cross over County Bridge and turn left down steps to follow a path beside the River Tees, then a farm access road. Pass the farm at **Step Ends** and continue along a track, then follow a path away from the river to reach a road. Turn left along the road, then right along a path, passing a farm at **Lonton** to link with the Tees Railway Walk.

Map continues on page 120

The old railway trackbed as it passes through the fields near Mickleton

Turn left to follow the old railway trackbed, passing fields and quickly crossing a fine five-arched viaduct over the **River Lune**, constructed in 1848. Cross a road to continue along the trackbed. When a stone-arched bridge is reached, there is road access to Mickleton, which has two pubs. The old station site is reached next, which also has road access to **Mickleton**.

The trackbed runs easily through pleasant countryside with views across the breadth of Teesdale. When the route approaches the old station near **Romaldkirk**, climb up to the right, then turn left down a road to reach the village, leaving the trackbed for a while.

Romaldkirk is one of the most attractive and interesting little villages in Teesdale. There are three greens and two pubs, fine cottages and beautiful gardens. An interesting 12th-century church incorporates a small amount of Saxon stonework, and has a couple of unusual features. One is a blocked-up north doorway, said to have the devil on the other side! Another is the tracery of the east window, which simply doesn't look right. Pevsner declared that it 'looks like a protest against all rules'.

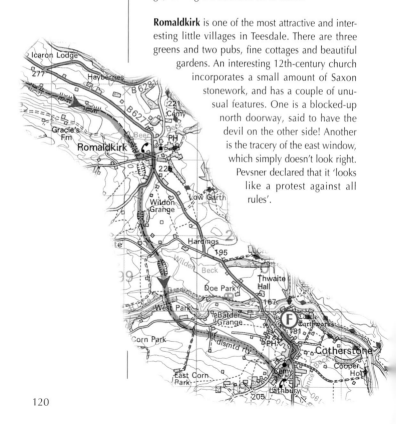

Turn right along the main road to leave Romaldkirk, as signposted for the Tees Railway Walk. Turn right again up the Hunderthwaite road. The old railway trackbed is seen on the left, signposted for Cotherstone. Follow the trackbed, crossing a minor road in a dip, then later a viaduct, constructed in 1848, over the River Balder.

Cross another minor road in a dip, then later go under a stone-arched bridge. When a road is reached, it can be followed into **Cotherstone** by turning left. Alternatively, walk a little further along the trackbed, then turn left down a narrow footpath to enter the village via the church. Turn left along the main road to explore the rest of the village, which has two pubs.

Cotherstone is a pretty little village that hardly cares to remember an old castle that once sat on nearby Hallgarth Hill. This 12th-century castle was occupied by the Fitzhughs, who were once the lords of Romaldkirk.

The old railway trackbed as it runs from Romaldkirk to Cotherstone

WALK 24
Middleton and Monk's Moor

Start/Finish	Middleton-in-Teesdale – GR 947 254
Distance	14.5km (9 miles)
Terrain	Easy woodland and valley paths, then exposed moorland tracks and paths
Maps	OS Landranger 92; Explorer OL31
Refreshments	Plenty of choice around Middleton-in-Teesdale
Transport	Regular daily buses serve Middleton-in-Teesdale from Bishop Auckland and Barnard Castle

A circuit of Monk's Moor reveals lead-mining sites at Hudeshope and Great Eggleshope. Nature is reclaiming the devastated dale-heads, and the once-busy mining paths and tracks are now quiet routes for walkers. Middleton-in-Teesdale was developed and controlled by the London Lead Company and was the headquarters of their Pennine operations. It takes a little imagination to appreciate what the mines would have been like in their heyday, with noisy engines, crushing mills, sterile spoil heaps and polluted waters. Hard work and loyalty to the company were rewarded with good housing, a decent wage and prospects for improvement. This route starts at an ornate black-and-white drinking fountain erected in honour of a past company superintendant.

Note an old arch in the graveyard while passing the church.

Walk out of **Middleton-in-Teesdale** by following the road, signposted for Stanhope, that runs uphill from the parish church. ◄ A narrow tarmac road branches left off the Stanhope road, and after a short walk along it, the King's Walk heads off to the right. This permitted path runs through delightfully mixed woodlands. Follow it along the woodland edge, turning right to climb uphill, then bear right at junctions to cross Snaisgill Beck using a footbridge. Follow the woodland edge down to a good track and look at the Skears Limekilns.

A path climbs above limekilns to follow Hudeshope Beck upstream

These **limekilns** were built between the early 18th and mid-20th centuries and operated until 1960. Limestone was quarried and crushed, then transported by a short railway to the kilns. Layers of limestone and coke were fired at 1000°C to make quicklime. 1000kg (1 ton) of limestone and 200kg (4cwt) of coke produced 650kg (13cwt) of quicklime. This was mainly for fertilising fields, but also produced mortar for construction and was used in lead smelting.

Keep right to climb past the kilns and discover the quarry that once fed them. Pass the quarry and climb steps, then continue along the woodland edge and enter fields. The path runs alongside the woods further up Hudeshope, then a gradual descent runs close to **Hudeshope Beck**. Continue walking upstream beside the beck. ◀ Pass rabbit-infested spoil heaps, where it is worth looking for minerals. The path crosses **Marl Beck** to reach a kissing-gate. Turn right to walk uphill and join a minor road.

The scars of old 'hushes' mark the hillside to the right, where dammed water was released to scour off the topsoil to reveal any bright seams of ore.

Old quarries and mining spoil are passed on the way upstream beside Hudeshope Beck

Turn right again to follow the road to a sharp bend, noting the vast gash of Coldberry Gutter across the devastated dale-head. Immediately before the sharp bend is a mining track on the left. Follow this uphill, noting that it swings sharply right, then left. (A public footpath is signposted straight uphill, if you wish to follow it.) On the right there is another track, passing through a gate and leading over from Hudeshope to Great Eggleshope. This is a plain and obvious track, crossing moorlands as high as 540m (1770ft), with small mining remains along the way.

The descent into Great Eggleshope is less apparent, so keep to the left of a small beck to avoid difficult ground. Watch for a small ruin on top of a spoil heap, and keep to the left of it to find a path leading to a stile in a wall. Turn right at the foot of the slope and go through a gate to pick up a track that follows Great Eggleshope Beck downstream. Ford this river then later cross a concrete slab bridge. Just before reaching a couple of derelict buildings, turn right and climb straight uphill.

A vague path leads to an old bell pit beside a stone wall. Cross a stile and head straight up a moorland slope. Actually, it is better to bear slightly right to exploit a grassy strip and keep off the heather. Pass to the right of a small, breached dam. Pass a white porcelain sink, and as height is gained, drift slightly left.

When a big cairn is seen on the rocky edge of **Monk's Moor**, keep well to the left to reach another cairn. A vague path runs past it, crossing the top of the moor at 565m (1855ft). However, this is all access land, and it is worth visiting the big cairn and walking along the rocky edge, passing an intricate sheepfold and a ruined shooting hut.

When heading roughly southwest down from Monk's Moor, note a line of grouse butts, and well to the left, a solitary cairn on a boulder. Pick a way between the butts and cairn, exploiting a grassy strip, and walk down to a wall. Turn left to follow the wall to a junction and cross a stile.

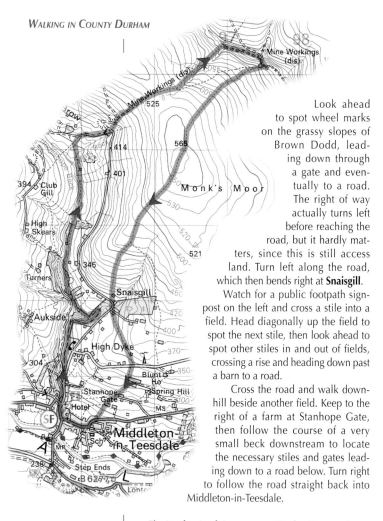

Look ahead to spot wheel marks on the grassy slopes of Brown Dodd, leading down through a gate and eventually to a road. The right of way actually turns left before reaching the road, but it hardly matters, since this is still access land. Turn left along the road, which then bends right at **Snaisgill**.

Watch for a public footpath signpost on the left and cross a stile into a field. Head diagonally up the field to spot the next stile, then look ahead to spot other stiles in and out of fields, crossing a rise and heading down past a barn to a road.

Cross the road and walk downhill beside another field. Keep to the right of a farm at Stanhope Gate, then follow the course of a very small beck downstream to locate the necessary stiles and gates leading down to a road below. Turn right to follow the road straight back into Middleton-in-Teesdale.

The **London Lead Company**, or 'Quaker Company', so named after the religious persuasion of its directors, dominated mining activities in Teesdale and far beyond. This region was formerly the world's greatest producer of lead, and the company provided a

stable continuity of employment and development for two centuries, from the 1700s to the 1900s.

The company superintendent lived in grand style at Middleton House, while loyal employees could expect good accommodation and access to education and other services. At one time, 90 per cent of Middleton's working population was employed directly by the company. Cottages on California Row were built after a large deposit of lead was discovered in 1849, the same year as the California gold rush.

A town trail reveals the former blacksmith's shop, corn mill, school and co-op. New Town was developed as a model housing estate. When Robert Bainbridge retired from the position of company superintendent, a public subscription raised the ornate black-and-white drinking fountain in the town. The fountain has a twin at the mining village of Nenthead in Cumbria.

Middleton-in-Teesdale is surrounded by high, sprawling moorland

127

WALK 25
Middleton and Grassholme

Start/Finish	Middleton-in-Teesdale – GR 947 254
Distance	13km (8 miles)
Terrain	Fairly good hill paths, then easy low-level paths
Maps	OS Landrangers 91 or 92; Explorer OL31
Refreshments	Plenty of choice around Middleton-in-Teesdale; ice cream and sweets at Grassholme Reservoir
Transport	Regular daily buses serve Middleton-in-Teesdale from Bishop Auckland and Barnard Castle

There are more paths and tracks for walkers than most maps care to admit. The Pennine Way, well known as the first of Britain's waymarked long-distance trails, runs between Middleton-in-Teesdale and Grassholme. Other routes are available as permitted paths, including a shoreline path beside Grassholme Reservoir and the trackbed of the Tees Valley Railway. A combination of all these routes offers an interesting, short circular walk. The shore of Grassholme Reservoir is one of many reservoirs opened to the public by Northumbrian Water, while the Tees Valley Walk along the old railway trackbed is one of several railway paths opened up for public use throughout County Durham.

Walk out of **Middleton-in-Teesdale** by following Bridge Street, which is signposted as the road for Brough. Cross over the County Bridge and go uphill a short way before turning right along a road signposted for Holwick. Immediately on the left is a Pennine Way signpost. Follow a track uphill, crossing an old railway trackbed to climb to a gate. Keep right and climb up a grassy track to cross the crest of Harter Fell well to the right of a landmark clump of trees on Kirkcarrion.

The dark clump of trees on **Kirkcarrion** is like a pivot to this circular walk. The trees are said to cover the tomb of a Brigantean prince called Caryn.

When the tomb was excavated in 1804, an urn of charred bones was discovered. The site has a mysterious atmosphere and is reputed to be haunted.

Pass through a wall on the crest of Harter Fell, then note that the descent can be a bit fiddly. Aim for a ruined barn and keep left of it, then go down to another barn and keep right of it. The farm of **Wythes Hill** lies across a shallow valley, and all the necessary gates and stiles fall into place if the small fields are crossed diagonally.

Pass the farm and follow its access road down to the B6276. Another path starts just across the road and runs down through fields to reach **Grassholme Farm**. Turn left on leaving the farm to follow a minor road across Grassholme Bridge. After a prolonged dry spell the ruins of an old double-arched stone bridge are seen amid mudflats.

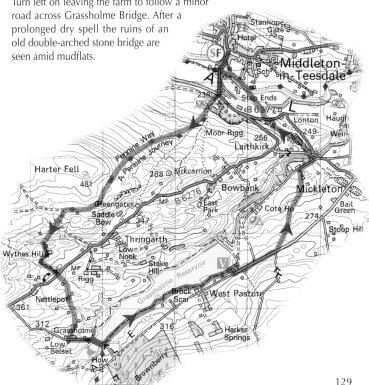

Climb steeply uphill from the reservoir, but only a short way, then turn left through an iron gate to enter the enclosure of **Grassholme Reservoir**. A pleasant shore walk runs between the reservoir and its stout boundary wall, and all the inflowing becks have footbridges. Before the dam of the reservoir is reached, pop into the **Grassholme Visitor Centre** for an ice cream. Taking advantage of the dark night skies in this area, the Grassholme Observatory was established in 2020. To make a booking, check the website www.grassholmeobservatory.com.

The first reservoir built in this area was **Hury Reservoir**. Construction began in 1884 in response to a huge increase in the population of Middlesbrough. **Blackton Reservoir** was completed in 1896, then work began on **Grassholme Reservoir** in 1910. Construction spanned 14 years and a tunnel was built to link with Hury Reservoir. Between 1950 and 1970, **Selset Reservoir**, **Balderhead Reservoir** and **Cow Green Reservoir** were built. Water from Lunedale and Baldersdale flows down pipelines to the Lartington Treatment Works, then is piped to consumers in Teesdale, Darlington, South Durham and Cleveland. Water from Cow Green simply regulates the flow of the River Tees and water is abstracted far downstream at Broken Scar near Darlington, where it may be mixed with water from Lartington. Untreated water is abstracted from the Tees even further downstream at Blackwell and Yarm for industrial use. Kielder Water's reserves can be used to augment the flow of the Tees via a subterranean aqueduct to the river at Eggleston.

Follow the access road up from the **Grassholme Reservoir dam** and turn left along a minor road. A short road walk leads to a signposted road junction, while on the left there is a footpath signpost. There is no trodden path across the field, so note the direction in which the sign points.

Go through the second gateway downhill, on the right, through a wall beside the first field, then follow the wall downhill. Go through a gate at the bottom and cross stone slabs over tiny Eller Beck. Turn right to go through another gate then walk uphill to Westfield House and continue along its access road.

Turn right to walk down a narrow tarmac road until a splendid five-arched railway viaduct comes into view. Turn left to walk across it, following the Tees Railway Walk. Continue along the old railway trackbed through a pleasant cutting. Turn right as indicated by a sign for Middleton and pass a farm at **Lonton** to reach a road.

Turn left along the road, then right to pick up a field path leading to the River Tees. Follow the riverside path upstream, past a farm at **Step Ends**, to reach County Bridge. Turn right to walk back up into Middleton-in-Teesdale.

Grassholme Bridge, close to where an older bridge is seen during droughts

WALK 26
Low Force and High Force

Start/Finish	Bowlees Visitor Centre – GR 907 283
Distance	11.5km (7¼ miles) or 12.5km (7¾ miles)
Terrain	Easy riverside paths, with moorland paths and tracks
Maps	OS Landrangers 91 or 92; Explorers OL19 and OL31
Refreshments	Café at Bowlees Visitor Centre; Farmhouse Kitchen off-route at Holwick
Transport	A very limited bus service serves Bowlees from Middleton-in-Teesdale and Langdon Beck on Wednesdays

The waterfalls of Upper Teesdale are truly magnificent. High Force is England's biggest waterfall, where the Tees breaks furiously over a dolerite cliff. Low Force is a less powerful, but attractively rugged cascade. Both waterfalls are easily approached from the B6277, and many casual visitors link them by following a riverside path that is part of the Pennine Way. If the walk from Low Force to High Force is extended, then Bleabeck Force can be included further along the Pennine Way. To create a circular walk, the Pennine Way can be linked with the course of an old drovers' route, the Green Trod on Cronkley Fell, to return to the village of Holwick. Low Force is seen a second time this way, and there is the option, if starting and finishing at Bowlees visitor centre, to include the nearby waterfall of Summerhill Force.

Housed in an old Methodist chapel, the **Bowlees visitor centre** offers background information and displays relating to the geology, history and natural history of Teesdale. There are plenty of notes about wildflowers, and some species may actually be growing in planted areas outside the building. There is helpful literature on sale, including plant guides specifically about the flowers of Upper Teesdale. There is a small café on site, tel 01833 622145.

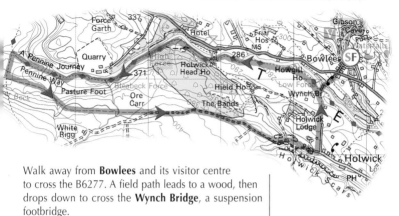

Walk away from **Bowlees** and its visitor centre
to cross the B6277. A field path leads to a wood, then
drops down to cross the **Wynch Bridge**, a suspension
footbridge.

*Low Force can be
admired at the start
and finish of the
walk near Bowlees*

133

This was the site of the earliest **suspension bridge** in the country, strung across the gorge in 1704. When it collapsed, it was replaced with the present structure. During a flood in recent years it was possible to lie down on the footbridge and touch the surface of the river beneath!

Once across the Wynch Bridge, turn right to follow the Pennine Way upstream alongside the River Tees, passing a sculpture of sheep and admiring waterfalls at **Low Force**.

The Pennine Way is surrounded by profuse growths of juniper as it continues upstream, and this is said to be the largest stand of juniper in the country.

There are other small falls and rocky gorges further upstream, then Holwick Head Bridge is passed and a short climb leads up through a gateway. ◀

Although the path is hemmed in by the juniper, the roar of High Force is heard on the approach, and spur paths lead off to the right to precarious viewpoints.

Enjoy the sight of the water of **High Force** pounding furiously over a rock-step and boiling in a turbulent pool before rushing through a deep and rocky gorge. This is all seen for free, while people down in the gorge have paid for access from the High Force Hotel.

Continue along the course of the Pennine Way, passing close to the top of **High Force** and heading through an area sparsely clothed in juniper. A noisy, dusty quarry lies opposite the waterfall of **Bleabeck Force**, which is itself seen on the left. After inspecting this charming little fall, continue along the path, crossing small footbridges and climbing uphill through an area of juniper that has been fenced.

The Pennine Way features flagstone paving in some parts. Watch for the point where the Pennine Way swings north, and turn left, or south at that point. A vague path beside a fence leads across a beck by a gateway. Just beyond is the Green Trod, a prominent grassy ribbon of track across rough moorland. A national nature reserve sign confirms that this is the right place.

High Force pours into a well-wooded, rocky gorge

Turn left and follow the Green Trod gently downhill. Cross a couple of becks and climb more steeply uphill alongside a wall. Later, cross Blea Beck using stepping stones. Pass a cairn on a knoll and turn left along a clear track flanked by fences. Later, turn right to cross a stile flanked by sheep sculptures, and follow another track dropping down into a rocky valley at **Holwick Scar**.

The track reaches a minor road just on the edge of the village of Holwick. Turn left to take the road away from the village, then immediately after crossing a cattle grid use a field path on the right to descend to Low Force and the Wynch Bridge. Cross over the footbridge and walk up through a wood to cross a field. Cross the B6277 and follow a minor road straight towards Bowlees and its visitor centre.

To see yet another waterfall, follow a nearby riverside path upstream from a car park. This runs along a firm surface and soon reaches Gibson's Cave – an overhanging lip of rock where Summerhill Force pours into a broad pool. Afterwards, retrace steps to the visitor centre to finish.

Many of Teesdale's dramatic landforms owe their existence to the **Whin Sill**. This enormous sheet of dolerite was forced into the limestone bedrock under immense pressure in a molten state around 295 million years ago. As the heat dissipated, the limestone in contact with it baked until its structure altered, forming the peculiar crystalline 'sugar limestone' which breaks down into a soil preferred by many of Teesdale's wildflowers. While weathering, the Whin Sill proves more resistant than limestone, forming dramatic cliffs such as Holwick Scar, Cronkley Scar and Falcon Clints. Where the Whin Sill occurs in the bed of the Tees, its abrupt step creates splendid waterfalls such as Low Force, High Force, Bleabeck Force and Cauldron Snout. The rock has been quarried throughout this part of Teesdale, generally crushed and used as durable roadstone.

WALK 27
Holwick and Hagworm Hill

Start/Finish	Holwick – GR 904 270
Distance	23.5km (14½ miles)
Terrain	Rugged, high-level, bleak and exposed moorlands, sometimes with vague paths
Maps	OS Landrangers 91 or 92; Explorers OL19 and OL31
Refreshments	Farmhouse Kitchen off-route at Holwick
Transport	None

The sprawling slopes of Mickle Fell could be said to extend from Brough in Cumbria's Eden Valley to Middleton-in-Teesdale in County Durham, and from Cow Green Reservoir to Lunedale. This is an immense area of bleak moorland with very restricted access at its heart. However, footpaths and bridleways may be followed any time, and some parts are designated access land. This route starts and finishes in the little village of Holwick, but is long and remote, with no useful facilities along the way. The Green Trod, an old drovers' route, is followed from Holwick to Cronkley, then a footpath leads over the moors from Cronkley to Hargill. The B6276 is used in Lunedale, then a bridleway is followed from Wythes Hill back to Holwick. This represents a long and hard moorland walk, best attempted in fine weather when plenty of time is available. Some paths are vague or lightly trodden so navigation needs to be good.

Holwick is a long and straggly village. Walk through it until the road suddenly turns right, and go straight through a gateway that is flanked by a bridleway signpost. A track rises up through a rocky valley at **Holwick Scar**, where clumps of parsley fern grow in abundance. The track turns to the right towards the top of this valley. Cross a stile flanked by sheep sculptures, then follow another track off to the left, fenced on both sides and climbing gently across the moors.

A signpost beside a gate suddenly indicates a point where a public bridleway veers off to the right. (Looking at a map, it seems sensible to short-cut along the track, and normally there will be no objection to this, since it crosses access land.) The bridleway, however, follows the

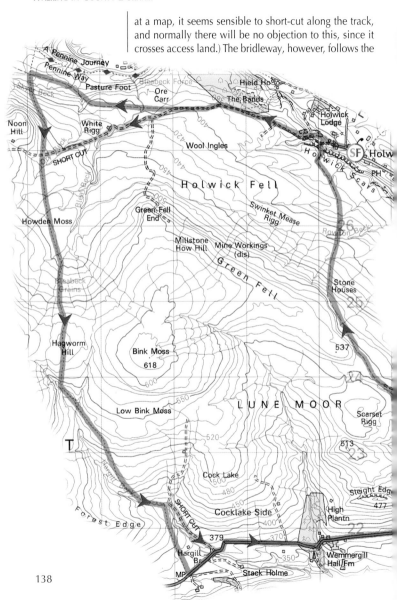

Green Trod, which is a vague moorland path that leads through another gate.

Pass a cairn on a knoll above a noisy stone quarry, then follow a drystone wall across a broad dip to cross stepping stones over **Blea Beck**. The track climbs over a low rise, then descends steeply alongside a wall and crosses a couple more becks. A gentle ascent leads to a national nature reserve sign. Turn left and ford **Skyer Beck** at this point, through there is no trodden path across the moor.

Climb uphill and keep to a slight break of slope to the left-hand side of the steepest parts of **Noon Hill**. The patchy moorland has been selectively burnt, and the route runs roughly southwards across it. Cross over the stony track that was being followed earlier in the walk, or if you arrive via the stony track, turn left instead. Either way, step across **Dry Beck** onto the moor.

There is no discernible path across the grass and heather moor, but there are a few waymark posts, and a national nature reserve sign indicates that the correct course is being followed. Look south across **Howden Moss** to spot a grassy ribbon of a path climbing towards Hagworm Hill. Walk towards this and climb uphill between Blea Beck and the line of a fence. A couple of cairns stand on the minor bump of **Hagworm Hill** at almost 600m (1970ft).

The grassy ribbon of a path leads downhill from a corner on the fence, then the heathery moorland slope becomes more stony on the way towards a tall and slender cairn. Keep an eye on the course of the path, which is vague in places, and it gradually it makes its way down to the confluence of Hargill Beck and Green Grain. Turn right to ford **Hargill Beck** and follow a track uphill. This levels out, and a vague path leads towards a large shed beside the B6276. (Alternatively, it is possible to follow the track directly to the road without fording the beck.)

The route starts and finishes at the rugged Holwick Scar

Turn left to follow the road across **Hargill Bridge**, then pass through woodlands at **Wemmergill Hall**. Continue past an old chapel, then a quarry where Robin Hood's Stone might be seen. Eventually, spot the farm access road for Wythes Hill on the left. Walk up the access road, which is part of the Pennine Way. Turn left at **Wythes Hill**, then pass another building behind the farmhouse, before leaving the Pennine Way by turning left through a gate.

Walk uphill alongside a wall, following a tractor track through a couple more gates, fording Merry Gill to climb past a ruined stone hut, keeping to its left. Walk uphill, using the course of a grassy track to cross **Scarset Rigg**. The track descends slightly to a couple of small black huts, where a left turn leads up a stonier track.

While heading towards the hump of **Green Fell**, be sure to bear to the right. A vague path runs across its slopes towards an area known as **Stone Houses**. It is possible to overshoot the point at which a descent should be made from the 500m (1650ft) contour, but this is no problem, since a wall runs down to a point where a gate allows **Rowton Beck** to be crossed.

A narrow path runs down a moorland slope to a gate in a fence. Go through the gate and follow a clear path flanked by numerous cairns. Follow this path through another gate, then drift to the right down through a rocky valley at Holwick Scar. ► Cross the steep-sided rocky valley and turn right along a track to return to Holwick to bring this long moorland walk to a close.

Again, parsley fern grows abundantly on the boulder slopes.

Holwick is a sturdy little village that was once the most northerly village in Yorkshire, before being annexed to County Durham. At the start of the walk, it may be possible to catch a glimpse of Holwick Lodge, which was built in the late 19th century. It looks palatial and is used by grouse-shooting parties, and is also said to have been used by the late Queen Mother on her honeymoon. Low Way Farm offers food and drink at the Farmhouse Kitchen, as well as cottages and a camping barn.

Looking back towards the moors from the road near Hargill Bridge

WALK 28
Mickle Fell via the Boundary Route

Start/Finish	Ley Seat, on the B6276 – GR 832 199
Distance	12km (7½ miles)
Terrain	High-level, exposed, bleak, remote, pathless, rugged moorlands
Maps	OS Landrangers 91 or 92; Explorer OL19
Refreshments	None
Transport	None

Access to Mickle Fell has always been fraught with problems. The high, rugged, exposed moorlands are difficult underfoot, and bad weather makes any trek to the summit quite arduous. The sprawling moors are used for grouse shooting, part of the fell lies within the Upper Teesdale national nature reserve, and the Ministry of Defence has staked out a vast 'Danger Area'. Those who manage Mickle Fell would prefer walkers to stay away, but walkers go there anyway, and an application can be made for permission to visit by contacting the MOD. The route offered is a straight-up and straight-down walk beside the boundary fence between County Durham and Cumbria, and is referred to as the Boundary Route. Walkers who wish to descend elsewhere must be prepared for a long walk over pathless, rugged, bleak and exposed moorlands. The MOD operates a free access information service – 0800 7835181 – or check www.gov.uk/government/publications/warcop-access-times.

Assuming you are armed with a permit, and that the red warning flag by the cattle-grid on top of the B6276 at **Ley Seat** is safely furled, then you can start this walk along the Boundary Route. Walk northwest from the cattle-grid, following the line of a stone wall. The wall marks the boundary between County Durham and Cumbria. Look out for occasional boundary stones inscribed with numbers – the one nearest to the road is number 46. The boundary changes direction slightly on the shoulder of **Hewits** at stone number 54, and a fence runs down into the Warcop Training Area to reach Connypot Beck.

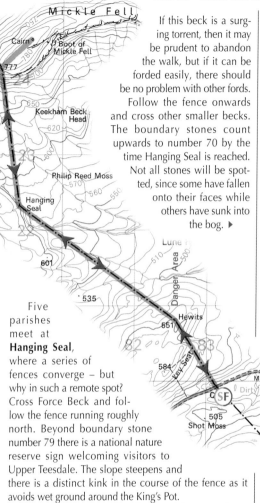

If this beck is a surging torrent, then it may be prudent to abandon the walk, but if it can be forded easily, there should be no problem with other fords. Follow the fence onwards and cross other smaller becks. The boundary stones count upwards to number 70 by the time Hanging Seal is reached. Not all stones will be spotted, since some have fallen onto their faces while others have sunk into the bog. ▶

Masses of cloudberries are evident on the squelchy moorland in the summer months.

Five parishes meet at **Hanging Seal**, where a series of fences converge – but why in such a remote spot? Cross Force Beck and follow the fence running roughly north. Beyond boundary stone number 79 there is a national nature reserve sign welcoming visitors to Upper Teesdale. The slope steepens and there is a distinct kink in the course of the fence as it avoids wet ground around the King's Pot.

When the fence reaches the top of the steep slope, head off to the right along the broad, grassy, level crest to a large bouldery **cairn** marking the summit of Mickle Fell at 790m (2591ft). Views are extensive, bleak

Observe the 'Procedure to gain access to the summit of Mickle Fell'

This is the highest point in County Durham and it is doubtless the wildest place in the county.

and desolate, taking in the north Pennine wilderness, Yorkshire Dales and distant Lakeland fells. ◄

The simplest descent involves retracing steps to Ley Seat. A descent north along the boundary fence can be considered if Maize Beck is running low, allowing a link with the Pennine Way, which could be followed either to Cow Green and Langdon Beck, or to High Cup and Dufton. There are discernible grassy wheel marks that can be traced from the summit of Mickle Fell to the lonely shooting hut of Silverband Shop, where a clear track leads to Holwick.

ACCESS TO MICKLE FELL

Procedure to gain access to the summit of Mickle Fell
taken from a notice posted at Ley Seat

1 Write to the Range Officer at Warcop Training Area, Warcop, Appleby, Cumbria CA16 6PA, with the date of your proposed walk, number in the walking party and your proposed route. (Please note: With regret it may not always be possible to grant permission for a walk on certain dates due to constraints imposed by military training, shooting, sheepherding or the risk of fire. It may therefore be prudent to provide several possible dates to the Range Officer when writing to him.)

2 The Range Officer will contact all the relevant landowners and game keepers on your behalf.

3 A permit and associated regulations will then be issued to you by the Range Officer.

4 Dogs, camping and the lighting of fires are not permitted on this ground.

WALK 29
Cronkley Fell

Start/Finish	Forest-in-Teesdale – GR 867 297
Distance	11km (7 miles)
Terrain	Some good tracks, but also exposed moorland paths and a rugged riverside path
Maps	OS Landrangers 91 or 92; Explorer OL31
Refreshments	None
Transport	A very limited bus service reaches Forest-in-Teesdale from Middleton-in-Teesdale on Wednesdays

Cronkley Fell is a mere bump on the wild, broad, sprawling slopes of Mickle Fell. It is managed as part of the Upper Teesdale National Nature Reserve, and a series of fenced plots across the top of the fell contain a wealth of rare and uncommon flowers. The fell can be approached from Forest-in-Teesdale, by using a short stretch of the Pennine Way. A grassy track known as the Green Trod leads over the higher parts of the fell, then a rugged path beside the River Tees can be used to return to Forest-in-Teesdale. If information about the range of flowers in Upper Teesdale is required in advance of this walk, then go to the Bowlees visitor centre (see Walk 26).

The rare spring gentian might be observed in May on this walk

Forest-in-Teesdale is a sprawling settlement, no more than a few farms and houses scattered among fields. A limited Wednesday-only bus serves the area and passes a car park below a school and a farmhouse bed and break-fast. Starting from the car park, turn right along the main road to spot a footpath sign, then turn left to follow a field path straight down towards a farm, keeping right of the building to continue down to the **River Tees**. A farm access track crosses a bridge and leads to **Cronkley Farm**, following the course of the Pennine Way.

Climb a rugged path behind the farm and cross a gentle rise, followed by a dip. The Pennine Way climbs gently uphill then swings left downhill. Don't follow it, but keep straight ahead, following a vague path beside a fence to cross a beck by a gateway. Just beyond is the Green Trod, which is a prominent grassy ribbon of track across rough moorland. A national nature reserve sign stands beside it.

The fenced enclosures protect the wildflowers growing on 'sugar limestone' from grazing by sheep and rabbits.

Turn right to follow the track uphill and later pass a sign announcing open access. The track leads over the broad top of Cronkley Fell, passing a series of fenced enclosures. ◄ Pass a spring at White Well and walk down past a cairn to follow a path down to the River Tees.

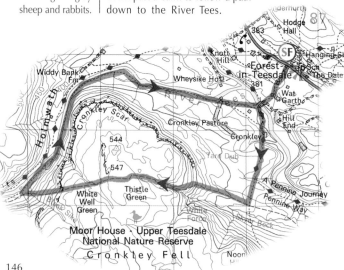

A fenced enclosure has been planted with juniper, and an island in the river is also covered in it.

Turn right to walk downstream. At first there is plenty of space for the path, but later the ground is rugged and the path narrow. Boardwalks have been installed in some places around the foot of **Cronkley Scar**, and there are views across the river to Widdybank Farm.

The path becomes wider and easier, passing a tumbled stone ruin. Continue, to reach a barn and go through gates to pass it. Follow a path through a field to reach a bridge that was crossed at the start of the day's walk. Cross it again and retrace steps up through fields to return to the car park below the school at Forest-in-Teesdale.

A bridge crosses the River Tees near the start and finish of the walk

WALK 30
Cow Green and Widdybank Fell

Start/Finish	Cow Green – GR 810 308
Distance	12km (7½ miles)
Terrain	Easy, though remote roads and good paths
Maps	OS Landrangers 91 or 92; Explorer OL31
Refreshments	None closer than the Langdon Beck Hotel
Transport	None

Widdybank Fell is an easy area to approach in search of Upper Teesdale's rare flowers. The walk round the fell uses minor roads and the course of the Pennine Way. Cow Green Reservoir dominates the start and finish, and while it is now part of the scenery, its construction caused howls of protest. The spectacular waterfall of Cauldron Snout is a fine feature on this walk. Walk round Widdybank Fell on a sunny day in the middle of May to make the most of its floral tributes. The spring gentian is at its best around that time and there are many more plants to see. Notice the outcrops of 'sugar limestone', which breaks down to form a crumbly soil that many of these plants prefer. Look for more wildflowers growing around the hay meadows of Widdybank Farm, which aren't mown until late in the summer.

The **Cow Green Reservoir** was constructed to slake the thirst of Teesmouth and its burgeoning industries. Sadly, an area rich in rare plants was drowned, despite vociferous protests, though some last-minute transplantation took place. The dam was built between 1967 and 1970 and holds 41 million cubic metres of water (9000 million gallons). The surface of the water covers 310 hectares (770 acres) and is 489m (1603ft) above sea level. Water is not piped away, but merely impounded and released as required, so that the flow of the River Tees can be regulated, allowing water to be abstracted far downstream at Broken Scar near Darlington for domestic use, and at Blackwell and Yarm for industrial use.

Start at **Cow Green** car park, checking information boards that display basic facts about the geology, scenery, flora and fauna of Upper Teesdale. Follow a nearby nature trail, which starts as a firm pathway but later follows the narrow minor road down past the enormous **Cow Green Reservoir** dam. ▶

Don't cross the bridge spanning the River Tees below the dam, but turn left along a flagged pathway to descend alongside **Cauldron Snout**, using the Pennine Way. A narrow gorge has been cut by the river, and the water boils furiously as it beats against the walls and tumbles over rock-steps. Step down carefully alongside, noting that the rock can be slippery when wet, and has been polished by the boots of previous visitors. Stand still if you want to admire the falls. After a final pyramidal outpouring, the Tees spreads out across a bouldery bed and rushes round a corner on its way to High Force (see Walk 26).

In spring and early summer, inspect the springy turf on the crumbling 'sugar limestone' beside the road, which supports a variety of wildflowers.

Looking down the spectacular cascade of Cauldron Snout

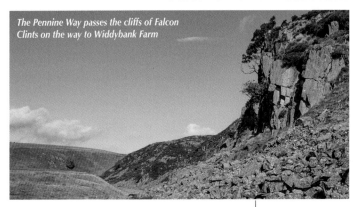

The Pennine Way passes the cliffs of Falcon Clints on the way to Widdybank Farm

The path continues as a flagged pathway hemmed in between the River Tees and the cliffs of **Falcon Clints**. ▶

Later, wooden boardwalks prevent boggy ground from becoming over-trodden. As the cliff-line dwindles, **Cronkley Scar** rears up on the opposite side of the River Tees. **Widdybank Farm** comes into view, one of the most remote farms in the region.

> Hay-making comes late around **Widdybank Farm**, compared to farms further down Teesdale, because of the altitude and resulting lower temperatures. Flowers growing in this area have a chance to ripen and drop their seeds before mowing takes place, resulting in self-regenerating, species-rich meadows. The farm is a base for Natural England staff working on the Moor House and Upper Teesdale national nature reserves.

Follow the access road away from Widdybank Farm, crossing the meadows and the rougher pastures beyond. Turn left along a minor road, which some call the Warden's Road, and follow it back over the moors, looking out for old mine workings, as well as a brick hut near the top of the road. A gentle descent leads back to Cow Green car park.

Ironically, the flagstones were quarried from the Pennines and used to build a mill, which was later demolished, with the stone being 'recycled' back into the Pennines.

Walkers pick their way across boulders beside the River Tees at Falcon Clints

The peculiar range of flowering plants thriving in Upper Teesdale, known as the '**Teesdale Assemblage**', owes its existence to a number of factors. The arctic/alpines survive because the climate in this bleak region suits them, keeping taller and more competitive plants at bay. The underlying crumbling 'sugar limestone' suits some species, while others grow on sodden, acid peat bogs. Plants that once grew in well-wooded areas now survive by adapting to life in the shade of boulders and cliffs.

Many will hear about the spring gentian, which is strikingly blue on sunny days in early summer, though few know exactly where to find it. Other species of note include the mountain pansy, alpine bistort, bird's-eye primrose, Teesdale violet and blue moor grass. These grow alongside the more commonplace wild thyme, tormentil, thrift and harebells, while wood anemones and woodland ferns have adapted to non-wooded habitats.

These plants are survivors from a bygone age, but also remind visitors how habitats have changed over long periods of time.

WALK 31
Cow Green and Herdship Fell

Start/Finish	Cow Green – GR 810 308
Distance	15km (9½ miles)
Terrain	Fairly easy moorland tracks and paths, but indistinct towards the end
Maps	OS Landranger 91; Explorer OL31
Refreshments	None closer than the Langdon Beck Hotel
Transport	None

A clear, firm mining track wanders round the western side of Herdship Fell, passing four distinct mining sites. On the Harwood side of the fell, an old road can be combined with vague footpaths to return to Cow Green. The route starts by conveying walkers into the huge, boggy bowl of Upper Teesdale, where there is a great sense of space and wilderness, but then the track suddenly lands on the B6277 on Harwood Common, where the sense of wilderness vanishes like a burst bubble. The walk around Herdship Fell is pleasant, fairly easy, and is likely to be quiet even when the circuit of nearby Widdybank Fell is busy.

Start at **Cow Green** car park, checking information boards that display basic facts about the geology, scenery, flora and fauna of Upper Teesdale. Follow a track marked as 'No Entry', which only applies to vehicles. Walk along the track, noticing signs of mining straight away. A fine view around Upper Teesdale takes in the sprawling slopes of Mickle Fell, the rounded Dun Fells and lofty Cross Fell.

Pass another mining area on **Backside Fell**, drifting away from the head of Cow Green Reservoir. A building on this site has been spared from ruin and serves as a shooting hut. One room is open, if shelter is required in this remote spot.

Continue further along the track to pass another mining area at Green Hurth. Follow the track above the ruins, where spoil heaps are infested with rabbits. Walk roughly

A room is left open for shelter at this shooting hut on Backside Fell

north along the final part of this track, where mining remains become smaller in scale and the surrounding moors become wilder and more desolate.

Follow the track as it winds alongside **Crook Burn**, giving the impression that it penetrates even further into the wilderness, although it actually lands suddenly on the B6277, one of the highest roads in the country at almost 600m (1970ft).

Turn right along the road, which runs gently downhill. Another right turn reveals the old road to Harwood, which drops steeply and gains a tarmac surface when it reaches Frog Hall and **Herdship**. At the next building, which is Watersmeetings, turn right to leave the road and walk across fields to reach a ruined chapel beside **Harwood Beck**. Cross a footbridge, then walk downstream to reach a minor road. ◀

In summer, masses of yellow globe flowers grow on the wet slope between the two farmhouses.

Turn right to walk up the road, then turn right again to reach **Binks House**. Keep left and follow a path climbing indistinctly across the moorland slope. The gradient eases and the path passes some small mine workings. Join a minor road, which some call the Warden's Road, at a brick hut. A gentle descent on the road leads back to the car park at Cow Green.

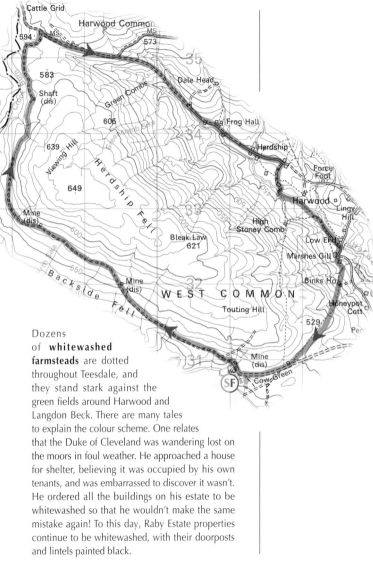

Dozens of **whitewashed farmsteads** are dotted throughout Teesdale, and they stand stark against the green fields around Harwood and Langdon Beck. There are many tales to explain the colour scheme. One relates that the Duke of Cleveland was wandering lost on the moors in foul weather. He approached a house for shelter, believing it was occupied by his own tenants, and was embarrassed to discover it wasn't. He ordered all the buildings on his estate to be whitewashed so that he wouldn't make the same mistake again! To this day, Raby Estate properties continue to be whitewashed, with their doorposts and lintels painted black.

WALK 32
Bishop Auckland and Binchester

Start/Finish	Market Place, Bishop Auckland – GR 212 302
Distance	7.5km (4½ miles)
Terrain	Easy low-level field paths, woodland paths and tracks
Maps	OS Landranger 93; Explorer 305
Refreshments	Plenty of choice at Bishop Auckland; pub at Coundon Gate
Transport	Regular daily buses serve Bishop Auckland, with the main ones being from Newcastle, Durham, Darlington and Weardale. Rail services run to Bishop Auckland from Darlington and Middlesbrough.

Newgate Street is the main shopping street in Bishop Auckland, and is based on the Roman road of Dere Street. A Roman fort lies to the north of town, near Binchester. The prince-bishops of Durham enjoyed a long-standing interest in the area, maintaining extensive parkland for hunting and for entertaining visitors. When a railway was being extended to Bishop Auckland in 1843, the bishop valued his privacy so much that he required it to be kept completely from his sight, even though it passed close to his residence! The comedian and actor Stan Laurel was a famous son of the town, for although he was born at Ulverston, he spent his formative years in Bishop Auckland, and had an interest in the theatre from an early age. A town trail includes several places associated with him and his family.

Start in Market Place in Bishop Auckland, which is dominated by the Town Hall. Walk down a road called Wear Chare to reach the banks of the River Wear. Turn right at a pumping station and follow a grassy bank beside the river, heading downstream parallel to a road.

Cross a road bridge, then follow a narrower grassy bank round a bend in the river. When a wood appears on the right, opposite a small lay-by, turn right to follow a woodland path. To visit nearby **Binchester Roman Fort**, stay on the road instead, climbing from the river to reach it as signposted, then return afterwards.

The Roman road Dere Street was built through northern England around AD80, with the fort of **Vinovia** constructed around the same time near Bishop Auckland. It was occupied for three centuries, and while built originally from wood, was later reconstructed in stone. It is open to visitors from May to September, tel 01388 663089, www.durham.gov.uk/binchester.

A woodland path runs parallel to Bell Burn above Binchester

Climb steps through the woodland to emerge in a field. Follow a fence through two big fields, turning left in the second field. The Roman fort is nearby, but there is no right of way to it across the fields. Watch for a stile on the right and walk down through a field to cross Bell Burn. Walk a few paces, then turn right to follow a woodland path gently uphill. Beeches are prominent and the understorey contains holly and brambles. Bluebells, wood anemones and garlic-scented ramsons grow beside the convoluted stream.

When an old railway arch is reached, turn right and climb up steps, then turn right to follow an old trackbed, which is now the Auckland Way. Walk under an arch, then later under another arch and go through a short tunnel – the latter was constructed to allow the Bishop of Durham to cross the railway without having to look at it! There are more open views, stretching away to distant moors, as the trackbed passes a golf course.

After passing the golf course, turn right to cross a stile (a left turn would lead quickly to Coundon Gate and the Top House pub). A field path runs alongside a stout stone wall that encloses **Auckland Park**. Follow the wall straight over a rise and down across the golf course access road towards Bishop Auckland. Follow a busy road across a dip, then turn right as signposted to return to Market Place in the centre of town.

Auckland Tower offers a bird's-eye view of the centre of Bishop Auckland

The Roman road Dere Street, running from York to Scotland, provided the foundation for Newgate Street in the centre of **Bishop Auckland**. The town is undoubtedly ancient, but gained prominence due to its association with the Bishops of Durham. Land was granted to the church by Canute around 1020, and monks from Durham cathedral founded a church in 1083. The town was always important for its market, and at one time a huge green extended from Bondgates to Market Place. Successive Bishops of Durham enjoyed hunting in the area, extending a manor house, then adding a banqueting hall, which was later converted into a chapel. When Bishop van Mildert gave up Durham Castle in the mid-19th century, Auckland Castle became his residence instead. Bishop Auckland became extremely prosperous, being on a busy coach road, while the bishops often entertained in grand style. Railways arrived in 1843, bringing further trade and industry to the town. The French-style château-like town hall dates from 1861. For other features of interest, check the Auckland Project, tel 01388 743750, www.aucklandproject.org.

The ornate entrance gate to Auckland Castle in Bishop Auckland

WALK 33

Circuit of Crook

Start/Finish	Market Place, Crook – GR 165 356
Distance	15km (9½ miles)
Terrain	Easy low-level field paths, woodland paths and tracks
Maps	OS Landranger 92; Explorer 305
Refreshments	Plenty of choice at Crook; pub at Billy Row
Transport	Regular daily buses serve Crook from Durham, Bishop Auckland, Darlington and Weardale

Crook is surrounded by low hills and fields, and is blessed with plenty of public footpaths. Wear Walking for Health and Durham County Council's Parish Paths Partnership worked with several bodies to identify and promote four short walks around the rural fringes of Crook, and these are combined in the following route description to make a complete circuit of the countryside close to the town. The four walks have been labelled according to compass points, and the order in which they are combined in this walk is east, north, west and south. The starting point is the attractively paved Market Place in the centre of Crook.

Start in Market Place in Crook and walk down the main road to cross Crook Beck. Turn left up George Terrace, a peculiar 'street' that has no road, just a row of houses. Turn right at the top and pass a row of garages, then turn left at Cemetery Cottages to follow a path straight uphill. Turn right to follow an old railway trackbed along the top of the cemetery. When a road is reached, turn left, then immediately right to follow the access road to Crook Golf Club.

Keep to the left of the clubhouse, then when two tracks fork, follow the one climbing to the left. When this bends left towards an enormous wind turbine, turn right along a narrow path and cross a tumbled stone wall as marked. Turn left to follow it, walking alongside a field, enjoying good views across Crook to the North Pennines. Cross a stile and keep straight ahead past an old quarry. Cross another stile, then after a slight ascent, cross another stile and continue

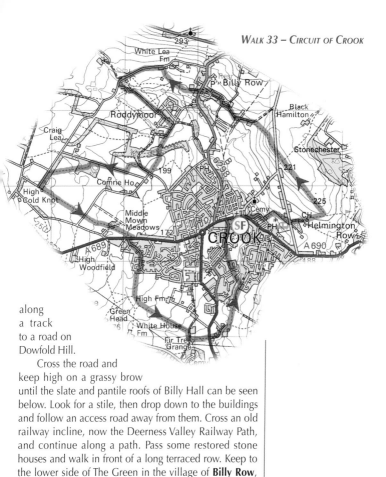

along
a track
to a road on
Dowfold Hill.

Cross the road and
keep high on a grassy brow
until the slate and pantile roofs of Billy Hall can be seen
below. Look for a stile, then drop down to the buildings
and follow an access road away from them. Cross an old
railway incline, now the Deerness Valley Railway Path,
and continue along a path. Pass some restored stone
houses and walk in front of a long terraced row. Keep to
the lower side of The Green in the village of **Billy Row**,
where there is a pub, shop and bus services.

Walk straight through a crossroads and pass Peases
West Primary School to leave the village. Follow a clear
track downhill, then climb to a road at **White Lea Farm**.
Turn left to follow the road across an old railway bridge
and pass some cottages. Turn left along a track signposted
as a public bridleway.

The track is quite clear and leads to a road and a
roundabout at some houses at **Roddymoor**. Turn right

161

A gentle path follows a wall along the crest of Dowfold Hill above Crook

along the road and continue along a dirt road to reach another tarmac road. Turn right again and keep straight ahead along a track, then turn left down a narrow path well before Roddymoor Farm. Cross a metal footbridge and climb up steps on a forested slope. Cross a stile at the top and follow a hedge straight to a road bend.

Don't step onto the road, but turn right along a clear path. Fork left along a lesser path, then turn left to cross a stile, walking straight ahead alongside a field to reach a road. Turn right to follow the road, which later runs alongside a forest, then turn left as signposted to follow a path leading through the forest.

Look ahead to spot stiles and walk through two fields to reach a belt of forest and another road. Turn left to walk along the road, then when the road turns right, turn left instead. Follow a straight field path, later crossing a road as signposted and passing a pond, gradually converging with the busy **A689** at a bus shelter.

Turn right to follow the main road, then left to walk through a housing estate, down Woodifield Hill and

Thistleflat Road. Climb and turn right along Sheridan Drive, then follow a short tarmac path linking with a field path. Walk straight downhill and turn left at the bottom, heading for a gate beside a holly tree. Go through the gate and follow a field path gently downhill. Turn right at the bottom to follow a farm road, then turn left along a footpath. Cross the busy A689 again at The Hollow and continue along an access road.

The parish church lies beside the Market Place in Crook

Walk to the end of a road at Low Beechburn, then cross a footbridge and walk uphill, bending to the left. Pass an upright railway sleeper covered in waymark arrows and head for a stile to follow a path to houses at Borrowdale Gardens, walking a short way along the road. Turn left down a flight of steps and cross a footbridge, then head up a path and track.

Turn right onto a tarmac path, which turns left to reach a road. Cross the road and follow the tarmac path straight to Glenholme Park and its sports facilities. Continue straight along the main road to return to the centre of Crook.

163

WALK 34
Wolsingham and Frosterley

Start/Finish	Market Place, Wolsingham – GR 076 373
Distance	16km (10 miles)
Terrain	Mostly easy field paths, moorland tracks and minor roads
Maps	OS Landranger 92; Explorer OL31
Refreshments	Pubs at Wolsingham and Frosterley
Transport	Regular daily buses serve Wolsingham and Frosterley from Bishop Auckland and Stanhope, along with occasional rail services

The Weardale Way is usually a low-level walk, but between Wolsingham and Frosterley it climbs high onto heathery moorlands. The so-called 'Elephant Trees' stand high on the moorland edge and are a landmark from all points around Weardale. A moorland track proves popular with walkers and cyclists, being broad and firm enough to accommodate both. Walkers can use riverside footpaths to return from Frosterley to Wolsingham, parallel to the Weardale Railway. The villages of Frosterley and Wolsingham are designated conservation areas. Frosterley's old quarries once produced decorative, fossil-rich 'Frosterley marble', which took a high polish and was greatly sought-after for monumental work. A town trail around Wolsingham could be enjoyed before or after this walk.

Wolsingham is a designated conservation area and a town trail reveals a wealth of interesting old buildings. Of particular note near the start of this walk are the Whitfield Cottages, formerly the Pack Horse Inn, bearing an old date-stone in Roman numerals that translates as 1677. Wolsingham was already an established market town in the dale, but in 1864 it also became an industrial centre when it acquired a steelworks. The parish church of St Mary and St Stephen lies in a quiet quarter of the town seldom explored by visitors.

Leave Market Place in **Wolsingham** as if going along the A689 to Stanhope, but turn left along a minor road signposted for Hamsterley. A bridge spans the River Wear and another bridge spans the railway, then the road climbs steeply uphill. Avoid a bend by taking the course of an old road, now a path, on the left.

Just before rejoining the road, go through a kissing gate on the left, then climb straight up through fields, watching for stiles and gates to reach **Chatterley Farm**. Turn right along the access track, then left uphill by road. Pass the access road for Rushy Lea, then keep bearing right along roads and tracks until the narrow road becomes a gravel track running beside moors high above Weardale.

Don't follow the track heading left to the isolated farm of **Harthope**, but go straight onwards through a gate to get onto the heather moorlands. A clear track is generally surfaced with sand or gravel and it never

The centre of Wolsingham is a designated Conservation Area

A track runs from fields to moorlands high above Wolsingham

The trees are known locally as 'the **Elephant Trees**' – you can decide for yourself whether they really look like elephants marching across the skyline when seen on the horizon from different parts of Weardale.

strays too far from a prominent boundary wall on the right. The track ascends very gradually on the heathery moor and passes a small plantation of beeches, heavily carved with the initials of visitors. ◄

Continue along the track to find a gate on the right where a clear track descends from the moorland. This is signposted as part of the Weardale Way. A track leads down to **Allotment House**, which is a large barn. A narrow tarmac road continues downhill, passing odd stands of trees.

The road leads through the tiny hamlet of **White Kirkley**, then climbs up to a road junction, passing old quarries on the way. Turn right at the junction and walk downhill again, passing a school and crossing a bridge over the River Wear and railway to reach Frosterley via the Black Bull Inn.

The substance known as 'Frosterley marble' is actually a dark and durable limestone that can be cut and polished in the same way as true marble. Unlike marble, the stone contains fossils, particularly

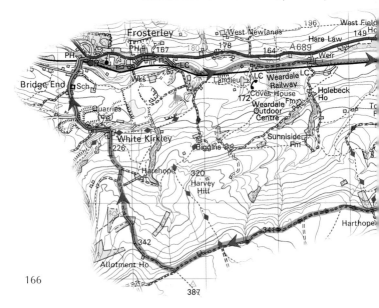

solitary corals, which create bizarre and intriguing forms when seen in cross-section. Look out for examples of Frosterley marble when visiting notable buildings around County Durham. Examples can be seen by making a detour into the interesting Harehope Quarry near Frosterley, harehopequarry. org, tel 07807 002032.

Looking back to the 'Elephant Trees' while descending past Allotment House

As soon as the main A689 is reached at **Frosterley**, turn right and walk along a narrow footpath. This leads round the back of the village, passing the parish church and wandering along a patchy tarmac road. Keep right to follow this road gradually down past Mill Cottages to a railway line. Don't cross the line, but turn left to follow a footpath and another road. Before reaching the main road, watch for a path squeezing past the left side of a row of houses. This leads close to a bridge over the River Wear.

Don't cross the railway line, but turn left and follow a path that runs between the River Wear and the railway. At first there is no access to the river, then a riverside path can be followed. When a **caravan site** is reached, follow its access road away to the next bridge. Don't cross the bridge, but continue straight onwards to follow a field path running parallel to a railway line.

Eventually, a flight of steps leads up to a bridge near a railway station. Turn left to cross the bridge over the River Wear, then turn right to follow a riverside path modified for wheelchair use through a caravan site to return to Market Place in the centre of Wolsingham.

The Weardale Railway has a station just outside Wolsingham

The **Weardale railway line** was constructed in 1847, by the Stockton & Darlington Railway Company, running from Bishop Auckland into Weardale, reaching Wearhead by 1895. Limestone was transported along the line to Teesside ironworks. A passenger service ceased in 1953, though freight continued from the cement works at Eastgate until 1993. The Weardale Railway Preservation Society was formed and trains now run between Wolsingham and Stanhope, though there is a long-term plan to offer services all the way from Bishop Auckland to Eastgate, www.weardale-railway.org.uk.

WALK 35
Wolsingham and Tunstall Reservoir

Start/Finish	Wolsingham – GR 076 373
Distance	12.5km (7¾ miles)
Terrain	Easy low-level walking on good paths and tracks
Maps	OS Landrangers 87 and 92; Explorers OL31 and 307
Refreshments	Pubs at Wolsingham
Transport	Regular daily buses serve Wolsingham from Bishop Auckland and Stanhope, along with occasional rail services

Most people wandering around Tunstall Reservoir drive there and either stroll around, picnic or fish. Those who walk from Wolsingham, however, can enjoy a fine walk around the Tunstall valley, as well as a walk round the shore of Tunstall Reservoir. Northumbrian Water allows access to the reservoir, while the land around the reservoir is managed as a nature reserve. The head of the reservoir is an important habitat for waders and wildfowl, while Backstone Bank Wood is ancient woodland. The village of Wolsingham is a designated conservation area, with plenty of fine old buildings worth inspecting.

Leave **Wolsingham** by following the B6296, called Angate Street, towards Tow Law, but when the edge of the village is reached, turn left into the Demesnes Mill picnic area car park. A path runs close to **Waskerley Beck**, modified for wheelchair use for just a short way. Notice a good viewpoint for a waterfall.

Follow the path upstream and pass a turning loop to continue along a field path, again tracing the beck upstream. After crossing a footbridge over Thornhope Beck, walk a little further upstream to reach an iron kissing-gate. Go through the gate and turn immediately left. A path leads away from the river and passes through a couple of fields to reach a minor road.

Cross the road and continue along a path straight up through more fields (don't follow the access road to

Fawnlees Hall). The path runs alongside a stout stone wall – watch for a glimpse of Fawnlees Hall beyond a fine line of trees. At the top end of the wall, cross a ladder stile to reach the ruins of a farmhouse called Park Wall, then turn immediately right through a gate.

An obvious grassy track runs around the edges of fields as it makes its way towards Jofless Cottage and **High Jofless**. After passing through the farmyard at High Jofless, turn left as soon as the road runs away from the farm. A field path leads towards a wood and the dam of **Tunstall Reservoir** is nearby.

Walkers could short-cut across the reservoir dam to shorten this walk, otherwise follow a road along the western shore, passing a toilet block by a car park. Stretches of shoreline path are available, but maybe stay on the road if these are busy with fishermen.

Continue to the head of the reservoir near **Tunstall House**. Cross the head of the reservoir by following a dirt road, then turn right to follow a path through Backstone Bank Wood. This is managed as a nature reserve and access is permitted by Northumbrian Water. Follow the woodland path, which is set back from the reservoir shore, until a track is reached climbing from the reservoir dam.

Turn left and follow this zigzag track up to the farmstead of Backstone Bank, which is a substantial old building. Turn right to follow a grassy track away from the farm, cutting across

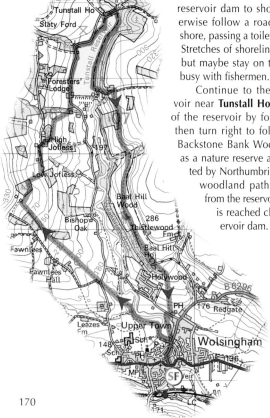

the valley slopes and passing along the top of a small forest nearby. Continue through a gate, then head down to Spring Gill Beck and cross over it. Climb from the beck and head straight across the next three fields, using gates to pass from one to the other.

Wolsingham is a fine Weardale village and its centre is a designated conservation area

Fishing boats moored beside Tunstall Reservoir

Pass along the top edge of Baal Hill Wood to reach **Baal Hill House**. Walk straight across a track at this point and go into a small wood straight ahead. A path leads down through the wood, continuing down through the fields below to reach a minor road. Just to the left is a holy well dedicated to St Aelric and St Godrick. Turn right along the road, then left to follow another short field path. This leads back towards the entrance of the Demesnes Mill picnic area. Simply walk back along the road to return to the centre of Wolsingham.

Tunstall Reservoir was constructed in 1879, but the water isn't used in nearby Wolsingham. Instead, it is piped well away from the valley to such places as Willington, Shildon, Spennymoor and Sedgefield. A small community at Tunstall was consigned to the depths, but Foresters' Lodge was built to replace one of the buildings. The farms of Tunstall House and Backstone Bank were high enough up the valley sides to be spared. Also spared was most of Backstone Bank Wood, a slope of ancient woodland that was once managed as a self-regenerating coppice wood. It is predominantly oak, though there are many other species present.

WALK 36
Stanhope and Stanhope Dene

Start/Finish	Durham Dales Centre, Stanhope – GR 996 392
Distance	15km (9½ miles)
Terrain	Mostly easy field paths and moorland tracks, but occasionally pathless with some steep slopes
Maps	OS Landrangers 87 and 92; Explorer 307
Refreshments	Pubs at Stanhope
Transport	Regular daily buses serve Stanhope from Wearhead and Bishop Auckland

Fine countryside lies north of Stanhope, where little fields quickly give way to quarried slopes, followed by open moorland. This walk climbs to Crawleyside by way of a quarried edge now reverting to nature. An old railway incline leads onto open moorlands, then the pleasant 'Velvet Path' runs down to a mining site in Stanhope Dene. Another climb leads to the fringes of extensive moorland, where the route runs easily alongside a forest. A final descent leads back down through fields to Stanhope Dene, and so back to Stanhope. Plenty of background information about this part of the North Pennines can be obtained from the Durham Dales Centre in Stanhope.

Start at the Durham Dales Centre in **Stanhope** and follow the main road straight out of town in the direction of Wolsingham. The last buildings are reached opposite the Weardale Travel bus depot. Turn left onto Woodcroft Gardens, then, after passing two bungalows, go right along a path that leads into a field. Continue straight ahead and cross a footbridge over a stream. Turn left and walk upstream, through a well-wooded valley.

The path climbs above the flow, then drops down stone steps to cross another footbridge. Climb stone steps on the other side, and partway up them, turn right along a narrow path and head further up through the wooded valley. Emerge from the woods to ford the stream, then follow a wall that runs parallel to the stream, fording it again at a stand of trees.

Climb uphill and pass above a few buildings at **Hill Crest** to reach a track. Cross the track and head straight across heather to reach another track, then turn right to follow it. There are walls on either side of the track, and on the left the wall heads downhill, while on the right the wall heads uphill. Follow neither, but watch for a path in between, traversing Crawley Edge on the fringe of a moor, overlooking buildings at **Crawleyside**.

The path approaches a road, but there is no need to walk on tarmac. Stay on the moor to pass the last building, then pick up a cinder-strewn track. ◄

Climb the incline, parallel to the road, passing a rectangular walled enclosure.

This was formerly a railway incline, which used to carry waggons between the Weatherhill Engine and the Crawley Engine.

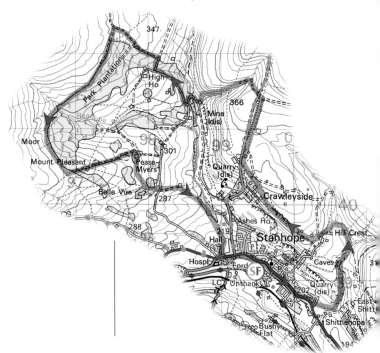

Afterwards, turn left to cross the B6278. A clear track runs down and round a moorland valley, passing a metal memorial bench. Part of this track is known as the Velvet Path, being covered in short green turf. The final descent is stony, and leads down through a gate to some derelict mining buildings in Stanhope Dene.

Turn right to follow a track to a bridge over Stanhope Burn. Cross the bridge, follow the track uphill and turn right at a junction. Follow the track further uphill until another junction is reached below **High House**. Turn right through a belt of woodland and go through a gate, then turn left to follow the track uphill. The track pulls away from the boundary wall and climbs to yet another junction on Stanhope Common.

Farm tracks and field paths descend to Stanhope Dene and Stanhope

Turn left and follow a track running beside the clear-felled **Park Plantation**, where only a straggly line of tall pines remain. The track diminishes as it progresses across the moorland slope. Pass a crater-like quarry and cross **Reahope Burn**. Climb uphill alongside the forest, then descend slightly on Reahope Moor, with a view into Weardale. Turn left through a gate, passing through a narrow part of the forest, then pass **Mount Pleasant**. Walk down an access track to reach another farm at **Pease Myers**.

Don't go down the access track, but turn right up through the farmyard, then left through a gate into a field. Walk straight ahead to spot a gate, then a stile, then head towards a house **Belle Vue**, turning left to go through a small gate as marked. Continue down through a field and cross a road.

Walk down an access track to reach a house at Widleyfield. There are two gates, so go through the one on the right and cross a field diagonally. Cross a stile in the far corner, then turn left to cross another stile and enter a wood. Walk a short way to join a path in Stanhope Dene and turn right. The path becomes a track, leading to a main road near **Stanhope Hall**, where a left turn leads straight back into **Stanhope**.

> **Stanhope** is a designated conservation area, and the parish church of St Thomas, with its 'fossil tree', dominates Market Place. The 'living' of this parish was once one of the wealthiest in the country. Rectors were entitled to a tithe of one-tenth on all the lead mined in Weardale, and could afford to live elsewhere in grand style, employing lowly curates to do their work. This was resented by most of the dalesfolk, especially those engaged in lead mining, and the spread of Nonconformism created plenty of local friction with the established church. The tithe was abolished in the 19th century. Note the stump of a fossil tree, genus Sigillaria, set into the churchyard wall. It was discovered in a nearby quarry and is some 320 million years old.

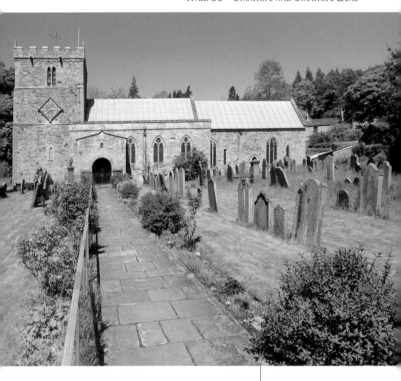

Stanhope Castle lies behind a wall, and few visitors are aware of its presence. It was constructed in 1798 and bankrupted the builder. A group of miners who were caught poaching grouse were locked up at the Bonny Moor Hen pub on their way to Durham gaol. Their comrades stormed the building, beating the keepers and constables who were on guard, and rescued the inmates. The event is commemorated in verse and no one was ever brought to trial. The Durham Dales Centre houses a tourist information centre, tel 01388 527650, www.durhamdalescentre.co.uk.

The parish church once provided its vicar with an impressive 'living'

WALK 37
Westgate, Middlehope and Rookhope

Start/Finish	Westgate – GR 907 381
Distance	16km (10 miles)
Terrain	Easy field paths and tracks, but rough and vague moorland paths
Maps	OS Landrangers 87 and 92; OL31 and 307
Refreshments	Pub at Westgate
Transport	Regular daily buses serve Westgate from Stanhope and Wearhead. Occasional weekday buses serve Rookhope from Stanhope.

Westgate, Eastgate and Northgate are place names in this part of Weardale – but there is no Southgate. The 'gates' marked the boundary of an ancient hunting forest frequented by the Bishops of Durham. The foundations of their hunting lodge can be seen near the road between Eastgate and Westgate. The following walk wanders through this ancient preserve, but concentrates more on mining and quarrying activities. The route climbs from Westgate over to Rookhope, returning by way of Northgate Fell. The ascent via Middlehope Burn reveals a delightfully overgrown lead-mining site, softened by nature, with waterfalls splashing alongside. After walking across moors around Hangingwells Common to reach Rookhope, an old railway trackbed can be followed back round Northgate Fell to return to Westgate.

Follow the Rookhope road out of **Westgate**, which bends to the right, then shortly afterwards a signposted track heads off to the left. Follow this track, then walk upstream beside Middlehope Burn, passing and old mill and a couple of lovely waterfalls. The narrow track is well wooded and leads to a more open area, passing the arches of a former bousesteads. ◄ The river has been enclosed in stone-built tunnels and it is quite possible to walk over its course without even realising. However, stay on the eastern bank of the river to continue upstream along a path.

A bousesteads is where untreated ore, or 'bouse', was stored.

After passing a small waterfall, another lead-mining site is reached, and the dark mouth of a level can be seen off to the right. Further upstream, the entrance arch to another level has a gate across it. A track crosses the path at this point, and by turning right, it can be followed up to another track. Turn left along this and follow it up to a minor road. Turn right along the road to reach **Scarsike Head**, which is a moorland gap. Don't cross the gap, but turn right down another road as if going back to Westgate.

Follow the road until a prominent track runs off to the left, flanked by walls. Walk along the track and go through a gate at the end of it. Head straight across the moors of **Hangingwells Common**, and try not to be confused at the number of vague paths trodden on the ground.

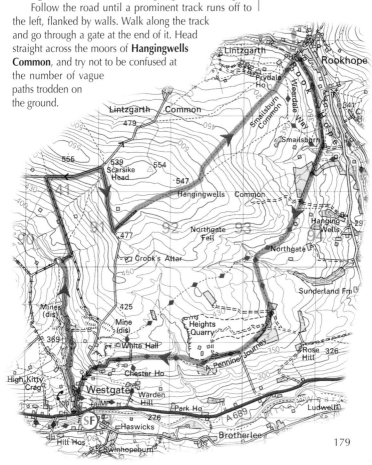

Don't worry too much about straying off-course, as either a stone wall or a wire fence will be reached before too long.

If the wall is reached, turn right, but if the fence is reached, turn left. A gateway stands where the wall and fence meet. Technically, the right of way crosses a stile nearby over the fence, though there is no trodden path to or from it. Either go through the gate, or cross the stile over the fence, then use the course of the stone wall running downhill to the northeast as a guide across **Smailsburn Common**.

The village of Rookhope will be seen ahead, and a small reservoir is passed before the final part of the descent. When a clear track is reached, there is an option to head into **Rookhope**, which has a shop, returning to this point later.

To continue the walk without visiting the village, turn right to follow the track, which accompanies **Rookhope Burn** downstream. The track follows the course of an old railway trackbed, climbing gently up past a small forest to reach a farm at **Smailsburn**. After passing the farm, a steeper stretch of the trackbed leads through another small forest, then the old line begins to level out as it crosses **Northgate Fell**.

Heaps of mining spoil spill into the river at Rookhope

The trackbed bends to the right and runs towards a prominent embankment, where it bends to the left and runs through a well-wooded cutting. Emerge from the cutting and cross quarry spoil to join the access road from **Heights Quarry**. Cross the road, then pass the quarry as marked to continue along the trackbed.

A viaduct once spanned Park Burn, but has been demolished, so walkers must descend to cross the stream, then climb. Further along, the trackbed has to be abandoned, so turn left, then right to join and follow a farm access road near Chester House. This leads down to a minor road, which is itself followed steeply down to Westgate. ▸

Part of this walk runs within an **ancient hunting preserve**. From 1430 the Bishops of Durham had a hunting lodge in Weardale, and its square platform site can be seen beside the road between Eastgate and Westgate. Such activities were frowned upon after the Reformation and hunting ceased. In earlier centuries, the Romans hunted in Weardale. Caius Testius Micianus captured a huge boar which no one else had managed to take, and erected an altar to Silvanus, the god of the hunt. A replica can be seen beside the road at Eastgate, and is one of many altars dedicated to Silvanus in this area. Travelling further back in time, the bones of exotic creatures long extinct in this country have been discovered in caves in Weardale, and it seems fair to assume that the earliest settlers also enjoyed the thrill of the chase.

A ruined farmstead seen from the old trackbed running around Northgate Fell

The railway trackbed from Rookhope ended with a steep descent to Westgate, with waggons hauled up and down by a winding engine.

WALK 38
Chapelfell Top and Noon Hill

Start/Finish	St John's Chapel – GR 885 379
Distance	13km (8 miles)
Terrain	Good tracks and paths on the lower slopes, but also rugged, exposed, pathless moorland
Maps	OS Landrangers 91 or 92; Explorer OL31
Refreshments	Pubs at St John's Chapel
Transport	Regular daily buses serve St John's Chapel and Ireshopeburn from Bishop Auckland and Stanhope

Wesley preached at Ireshopeburn between 1750 and 1790. He had a high regard for Pennine dalesfolk, and Methodist chapels are abundant throughout the area. Trekking over from Teesdale, Wesley noted that 'from the top of an enormous mountain we had a view of Weardale. It is a lovely prospect; the green, gently rising meadows and fields, on both sides of the little river as clear as crystal, were sprinkled all over with innumerable little houses'. Surely the 'enormous mountain' was Chapelfell Top, and this route features a stone in the shape of a chair, which offers just such a prospect. Rights of way lead from Weardale towards Chapelfell Top and Noon Hill, but expire on the moorland slopes. However, the moors feature designated open access, and a link between the two summits uses a fence as a guide.

In the village of **St John's Chapel** there is a small church is dedicated to St John. A bridleway sign nearby points across the road and reveals a track behind the Golden Lion pub. This track is easy to follow as it zigzags uphill, and wet patches alongside are rich in marsh marigolds and lady's mantle. Pass the whitewashed farmhouse of **Thatch Mires** and keep climbing.

When another track is reached, turn right to continue uphill, noting mountain pansies in early summer. A gate at the end of the track leads onto open moorland, where a large container serves as a storage shed. The public bridleway expires near here, but the high moorlands feature designated open access and can usually be explored further.

Leave the track and aim for the corner of a wall seen on the skyline. The gradient eases above the wall, then steepens again, and a cairn should be spotted above a boulder-strewn slope. Pass it to continue climbing and reach a small cairn on the broad, peaty summit of **Chapelfell Top** at 703m (2306ft). There are views beyond Weardale and Teesdale, but the sprawling moorland slopes obscure the dale bottoms.

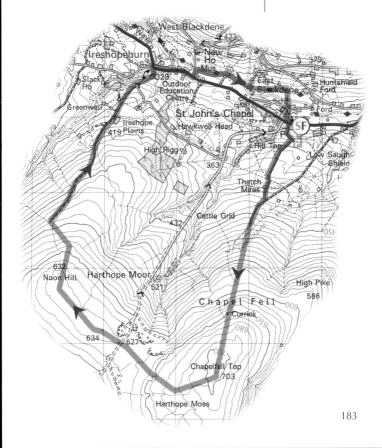

The long and straggly village of St John's Chapel in Weardale

Note the coir bolster
dams in the groughs,
placed there to
prevent erosion..

Keep walking across the peat hags and groughs to
reach a wire fence, and look out for cloudberry growing
among the heather, bilberry and lingonberry. Turn right to
follow the fence across the moors, wandering away from it
to find the best way through the hags and groughs, ◀ aim-
ing to reach a minor road at a cattle-grid at Harthope Cross.

The road runs at an altitude of 627m (2056ft) and is
one of the highest roads in the country. Cross over it and
cross a cattle grid to continue following the fence, passing above an old 'ganister' quarry, where tiered beds of
hard sandstone can be seen. There is hardly any ascent
worth mentioning as the fence continues to **Noon Hill**.
Fences meet on the grassy summit and the route passes
through a gate. Turn right to follow a fence down to a
wall, then turn left to follow the wall to an old railway
carriage that now serves as a storage shed.

A clear, walled track is another public bridleway,
offering a direct descent from the moors. Follow the track
downhill, and it later becomes a tarmac road at the farm
of **Ireshope Plains**, continuing down into the village of
Ireshopeburn. Turn right along the A689 and follow it to
the **Weardale Museum**. Either visit the museum or continue
the walk by following a minor road across the River Wear.

High House Chapel was built in 1760 and claims to be the second oldest Methodist chapel still in use. The **Weardale Museum** is in the former minister's house. Exhibits celebrate the life, work and history of Weardale, and one room is devoted to Wesley, who preached to the dalesfolk from a corner on the road outside, where a memorial now stands. The museum was established as a local venture, winning a Carnegie 'Interpret Britain' award. The trackbed of the Weardale Extension Railway passes between the museum and the River Wear and was constructed in 1895. Unfortunately it came too late for the lead-mining industry, which was already in terminal decline. Tel 01388 335085, weardale museum.org.uk.

After crossing the River Wear, turn right along a riverside path, which is part of the Weardale Way. Follow the path past two footbridges, maybe making a slight detour to visit a fine waterfall, then cross over another footbridge further downstream. A path leads to a road, which in turn leads to the main road in the middle of St John's Chapel.

A delightful little waterfall can be visited between Ireshopeburn and St John's Chapel

WALK 39
Cowshill, Killhope and Allenheads

Start/Finish	Cowshill – GR 855 406
Distance	17km (10½ miles) or 18.5km (11½ miles)
Terrain	Easy riverside paths, then exposed, high-level moorland tracks and paths
Maps	OS Landranger 87; Explorer OL31
Refreshments	Cafés at Killhope and Allenheads; pubs at Allenheads and Cowshill
Transport	Regular daily buses serve Cowshill from Bishop Auckland and Stanhope, and will occasionally run to Killhope on request. Buses also serve Allenheads from Hexham.

This walk features an interesting high-level loop that straddles the heads of Weardale in County Durham and Allendale in Northumberland, including several lead-mining sites. A fiddly series of riverside paths are used between Cowshill and Killhope. There is a splendid lead-mining museum at Killhope, but it takes time to explore properly, and if a visit cannot be made during the walk, then be sure to return some other time to do it justice. A track known as the Carriers Way is followed from Killhope to Allenheads, and on the way there is an option to detour to the summit of Killhope Law. Allenheads is a small village that has completely revitalised itself and boasts a fine heritage centre. A road and moorland paths are used to cross from Allenheads in Northumberland back to Cowshill in County Durham.

Start at **Cowshill** by following a minor road downhill to cross Burtreeford Bridge. Turn right to start following a path upstream, as indicated by a Weardale Way marker. An old flooded quarry can be seen on the opposite bank of the river, then the path rises gradually uphill beyond the next farm.

Later, drift back down to the river and cross a bridge at **Cornriggs**, and follow a path further upstream. When another bridge is reached, don't cross it, but bear right

away from the river to climb up to the A689 at **Slit Foot**.
Turn left to follow the road to the lead mining centre.

Killhope Wheel is the centrepiece
of the remarkable **North of
England Lead-Mining Museum**.
The overshot wheel powered
machinery in a crushing
mill and measures 10m
(33ft) in

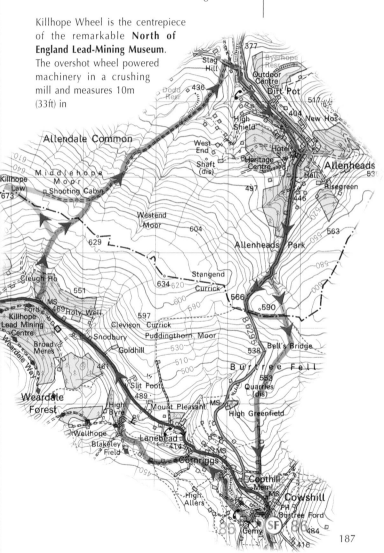

187

diameter. Ore came from the Park Level, which can be entered on guided tours. The bousesteads and washing floor have been restored, and feature plenty of 'hands-on' exhibits. Buildings have been restored and the mine 'shop' is of particular interest. Downstairs is a smithy and stable, while upstairs is a reconstruction of the sleeping quarters, though without the filthy, damp, smelly conditions which once prevailed. Some farmers worked in the mine, and some miners also worked on farms. There is a café on site, as well as a good range of background publications. If time isn't available for a thorough exploration, be sure to return at a later date. Tel 01388 537505, killhope.org.uk.

To continue the walk, cross over the road from the main entrance to **Killhope Lead Mining Centre** and follow a rugged path up through a clear-felled forest, replanted with native saplings. Further uphill lie open moorland slopes, where the Carriers Way passes a curious lead sculpture. The path reaches an altitude of 625m (2050ft), and some walkers may wish to detour off to the west to reach the summit of **Killhope Law**, at 673m (2207ft). A stout cairn, trig point and a wooden mast stand there, offering splendid views around the North Pennines.

Crushed ore from Killhope was hauled by pack ponies along the **Carriers Way**, over the moors to Allenheads. The ore was smelted at Slag Hill just outside the village, and sulphurous fumes were conducted up a long stone-built flue on the moorland slopes of Killhope Law. The flue was periodically swept out to ensure that nothing went to waste.

For the descent, simply link with a clear track running downhill from a shooting cabin on the hillside. The track runs parallel to the remains of an old flue, which can be traced downhill past **Dodd Reservoir** to reach the ruins of an old smelting mill at **Slag Hill**. Join a road at this point, and turn right to cross a bridge, then go right again.

Follow a road through the long and straggly village of **Allenheads** to reach the Allenheads heritage centre. Nearby Allenheads Inn, built in 1770, provides accommodation and houses articles from bygone ages.

Killhope Wheel is the centrepiece of an extensive and interesting lead-mining museum

Mining waggons arranged in front of the Allenheads Inn

Allenheads was a major centre for the Blackett-Beaumont family mining concern, known as WB Lead. The family held mining leases for two centuries from 1696. Aside from mining vast quantities of lead, a single silver nugget of 340kg (12,000 ounces) was also unearthed! Allenheads Hall was the family's summer residence. In recent decades Allenheads was in serious decline, but it was decided to capitalise on its heritage, and the village is now thriving. Visit the heritage centre and the Hemmel, the latter being a café in an old byre. The Blacksmith's Shop has exhibits relating to the geology, history and wildlife of the area. An enormous Armstrong hydraulic engine originally provided power for Allenheads, and was eventually brought back 'home' after being moved out of the area. Tel 01434 685119.

A rugged short-cut on the left is signposted as a 'restricted byway', leading directly across the moor.

Follow the B6295 uphill from Allenheads, as if crossing over into Weardale. ◄ The road exploits a high moorland gap at 587m (1926ft). Turn left through a gate at this point and follow a path uphill beside a wall. Don't go all the way to the top of **Burtree Fell**, but turn right through a gateway as marked.

Simply follow the line of a fence downhill, joining a much clearer track, which is enclosed in lower pastures. Follow the track down onto the A689 and turn left to return to Cowshill.

WALK 40
Edmundbyers and Edmundbyers Common

Start/Finish	Edmundbyers – GR 017 501
Distance	13km (8 miles)
Terrain	Mostly easy tracks and paths up through fields, then back across exposed moorlands
Maps	OS Landranger 87; Explorer 307.
Refreshments	Pub at Edmundbyers
Transport	Occasional weekday buses serve Edmundbyers from Consett

Edmundbyers is a quiet little Derwentside village arranged around a large green. The walk starts close to the parish church of St Edmund, and follows tracks and paths up through pleasant meadows and pastures, passing derelict farmsteads to reach heather moorland above the Ramshaw valley. The return to Edmundbyers takes a parallel course, but is almost entirely across moorland, and so presents quite a different aspect. The route described is also a loop on the Lead Mining Trail, which stretches all the way from Cowshill, at the head of Weardale, over to Edmundbyers. Lead mining becomes more apparent on the upper part of this particular walk, where the chimneys of old mines come into view in the Ramshaw valley.

Follow the B6278 out of **Edmundbyers** in the direction of Stanhope. Pass St Edmund's Church and head downhill towards a bridge, but do not cross it. Instead, turn right at a sharp bend before the bridge and follow a track. Don't follow this track up to a farm, but turn left along another track across a slope of gorse and bracken, roughly parallel to **Burnhope Burn**.

A good track is reached later, where a right turn leads up past the old farmstead of **College**. The track continues rising gently to go through another farmyard at **Pedam's Oak**. Apparently there was once a hollow oak tree here, and a horse thief named Pedam hid inside it to avoid being caught.

A clear and obvious track approaches the ruined farmstead of Pedam's Oak

The track descends slightly, then climbs up through fields again to pass the old farmstead of **Belmount**. Keep above this site to follow a track, which in turn follows a wall gently up onto open moorland. Bear gradually to the right on this track to reach a moorland road at 440m (1445ft). The Lead Mining Trail continues across Bolt's Law, but to return to Edmundbyers, turn right along the road, then turn right to leave the road as signposted.

The way across the moorland starts by following a clear track. Later, leave the track by turning right as indicated by a marker post, following a path. Go through the gate and continue walking gently downhill, following the broadest track across the moor. Another gate at **Chop Hardy** marks a transition from heather moorland to predominantly grassy moorland, but the track passes back onto heather moorland at another gate.

Continue to trace the broad and grassy track across the moors, still descending gradually. There is a bend in the track where it passes grouse-shooting butts and crosses a stream, then the route runs below an isolated field system on Edmundbyers Common. After crossing another stream the track joins a road and a short descent leads back into Edmundbyers.

Edmundbyers is a quiet little village with no facilities beyond a pub and youth hostel. The hostel was once a pub called the Low House Inn. It stood at a strategic point on packhorse ways, catching passing trade

from Tynedale, Allendale and Weardale. It is reputed to be haunted by the ghost of a former landlord, who died of exposure while searching the moors for his wife, who had gone missing. St Edmund's Church still has a little Saxon and Norman stonework incorporated into its more recently 'restored' fabric. The altar stone is unusual, in that it is made of a single slab of stone of a type forbidden following the Reformation. The slab was removed, but not destroyed. It was buried in the churchyard, where it was rediscovered in 1855, and has since been restored to its original position in the church.

Looking ahead across the moors on the way back to Edmundbyers

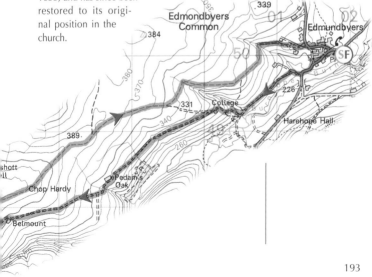

APPENDIX A
Route summary table

No	Name	Start (Finish)	Distance	Page
Routes				
1	Durham City and the River Wear	Durham Cathedral	5km (3 miles)	32
2	Bearpark, Broompark and Brandon	Ushaw Moor	12km (7½ miles)	36
3	Dipton and Hamsterley Mill	Dipton	9km (5½ miles)	41
4	Beamish and Causey	Beamish	110km (6¼ miles)	44
5	Ouston and Urpeth	Ouston	7km (4 miles)	49
6	Lumley Castle and Great Lumley	Chester-le-Street	11.5km (7 miles)	51
7	Durham Coast Path	Seaham (Hart Station)	20km (12½ miles)	55
8	Castle Eden Dene	Horden	13.5km (8½ miles))	62
9	Wingate and Station Town	Wingate	9km (5½ miles)	67
10	Cassop and Quarrington	Cassop	8km (5 miles)	70
11	Sedgefield and Hardwick Hall	Sedgefield	8.5km (5¼ miles) or 12.5km (7¾ miles)	74
12	Middleton One Row and Girsby	Middleton One Row	14km (9 miles)	78
13	Low and High Coniscliffe	Broken Scar	12km (7½ miles)	81
14	Gainford and Piercebridge	Gainford Cross	19.5km (12 miles)	84
15	Cockfield Fell and Butterknowle	Cockfield	11km (7 miles)	88
16	Woodland and Copley	Woodland	8.5km (5 miles)	92
17	Staindrop and Cleatlam	Staindrop	9km (5½ miles)	95
18	Greta Bridge and Brignall Banks	Greta Bridge	11km (7 miles) or 15km (9 miles)	99
19	Tan Hill and Sleightholme Moor	Tan Hill Inn	14km (9 miles)	102

20	Bowes and Bowes Moor	Bowes	16km (10 miles)	105
21	Barnard Castle and the Tees	Barnard Castle	12km (7½ miles)	110
22	Cotherstone and Romaldkirk	Cotherstone	10km (6¼ miles)	114
23	Tees Railway Walk	Middleton-in-Teesdale (Cotherstone)	11km (7 miles)	118
24	Middleton and Monk's Moor	Middleton-in-Teesdale	14.5km (9 miles)	122
25	Middleton and Grassholme	Middleton-in-Teesdale	13km (8 miles)	128
26	Low Force and High Force	Bowless Visitor Centre	11.5km (7¼ miles) or 12.5km (7¾ miles)	132
27	Holwick and Hagworm Hill	Holwick	23.5km (14½ miles)	137
28	Mickle Fell via the Boundary Route	Ley Seat	12km (7½ miles)	142
29	Cronkley Fell	Forest-in-Teesdale	11km (7 miles)	145
30	Cow Green and Widdybank Fell	Cow Green	12km (7½ miles)	148
31	Cow Green and Herdship Fell	Cow Green	15km (9½ miles)	153
32	Bishop Auckland and Binchester	Bishop Auckland	7.5km (4½ miles)	156
33	Circuit of Crook	Crook	15km (9½ miles)	160
34	Wolsingham and Frosterley	Wolsingham	16km (10 miles)	164
35	Wolsingham and Tunstall Reservoir	Wolsingham	12.5km (7¾ miles)	169
36	Stanhope and Stanhope Dene	Stanhope	15km (9½ miles)	173
37	Westgate, Middlehope and Rookhope	Westgate	16km (10 miles)	178
38	Chapelfell Top and Noon Hill	St John's Chapel	13km (8 miles)	182
39	Cowshill, Killhope and Allenheads	Cowshill	17km (10½ miles) or 18.5km (11½ miles)	186
40	Edmundbyers and Edmundbyers Common	Edmundbyers	13km (8 miles)	191

Countryside contacts

Durham County Council
The council website contains a wealth of information and contact details,
www.durham.gov.uk

Countryside Rangers
For details of guided walks, picnic sites, railway paths and events,
www.durham.gov.uk/countryside

Open Access Contact Centre
To check open access in advance,
tel 0300 0602091

Moor House and Upper Teesdale National Nature Reserves
tel 01833 622374

North Pennines AONB Partnership
For North Pennines information,
tel 01388 528801,
www.northpennines.org.uk

Durham Heritage Coast
tell 03000 268131,
www.durhamheritagecoast.org

Darlington Borough Council
www.darlington.gov.uk

Sustrans
2nd Floor Higham House,
Higham Place, Newcastle upon Tyne
NE1 8AF
tel 0191 2616160,
www.sustrans.org.uk.

Public transport contacts

Teesside International Airport
www.teessideinternational.com

Newcastle Airport
www.newcastleairport.com

DFDS Seaways, Newcastle
www.dfds.com

Traveline
tel 0871 2002233,
www.traveline.info

National Express Coaches
www.nationalexpress.com

LNER
www.lner.co.uk

CrossCountry Trains
www.crosscountrytrains.co.uk

Northern
wwww.northernrailway.co.uk

Arriva Bus,
www.arrivabus.co.uk

Go-North East Bus,
www.gonortheast.co.uk

Weardale Travel,
www.weardale-travel.co.uk

North East Explorer Tickets
networkonetickets.co.uk

Tourist information contacts

Durham City
tel 03000 262626,
www.thisisdurham.com

Seaham
Visitor Information
Dalton Park

Barnard Castle
Information Point,
The Witham,
Horsemarket

Sedgefield
Visitor Information
Hardwick Park

Bishop Auckland
tel 01388 743750,
www.aucklandproject.org

Stanhope
tel 01388 527650,
www.durhamdalescentre.co.uk

Visitor centre contacts

Durham Cathedral
tel 0191 3868669,
www.durhamcathedral.co.uk

Beamish Museum
tel 0191 3704000,
www.beamish.org.uk

Head of Steam, Darlington Railway Museum
tel 01325 405060,
www.head-of-steam.co.uk

Killhope – the North of England Lead Mining Museum
tel 01388 537505,
killhope.org.uk

Weardale Museum of High House Chapel
tel 01388 335085,
weardalemuseum.org.uk

Bowes Museum
tel 01833 690606,
www.thebowesmuseum.org.uk

LISTING OF CICERONE UK GUIDES

BRITISH ISLES CHALLENGES, COLLECTIONS AND ACTIVITIES

Cycling Land's End to John o' Groats
The Big Rounds
The Book of the Bivvy
The Book of the Bothy
The Mountains of England & Wales:
  Vol 1 Wales
  Vol 2 England
The National Trails
Walking The End to End Trail

SCOTLAND

Ben Nevis and Glen Coe
Cycle Touring in Northern Scotland
Cycling in the Hebrides
Great Mountain Days in Scotland
Mountain Biking in Southern and Central Scotland
Mountain Biking in West and North West Scotland
Not the West Highland Way Scotland
Scotland's Best Small Mountains
Scotland's Mountain Ridges
Skye's Cuillin Ridge Traverse
The Borders Abbeys Way
The Great Glen Way
The Great Glen Way Map Booklet
The Hebridean Way
The Hebrides
The Isle of Mull
The Isle of Skye
The Skye Trail
The Southern Upland Way
The Speyside Way
The Speyside Way Map Booklet
The West Highland Way
The West Highland Way Map Booklet
Walking Ben Lawers, Rannoch and Atholl
Walking in the Cairngorms
Walking in the Pentland Hills
Walking in the Scottish Borders
Walking in the Southern Uplands
Walking in Torridon
Walking Loch Lomond and the Trossachs

Walking on Arran
Walking on Harris and Lewis
Walking on Jura, Islay and Colonsay
Walking on Rum and the Small Isles
Walking on the Orkney and Shetland Isles
Walking on Uist and Barra
Walking the Cape Wrath Trail
Walking the Corbetts
  Vol 1 South of the Great Glen
  Vol 2 North of the Great Glen
Walking the Galloway Hills
Walking the Munros
  Vol 1 – Southern, Central and Western Highlands
  Vol 2 – Northern Highlands and the Cairngorms
Winter Climbs Ben Nevis and Glen Coe
Winter Climbs in the Cairngorms

NORTHERN ENGLAND ROUTES

Cycling the Reivers Route
Cycling the Way of the Roses
Hadrian's Cycleway
Hadrian's Wall Path
Hadrian's Wall Path Map Booklet
The C2C Cycle Route
The Coast to Coast Walk
The Coast to Coast Map Booklet
The Pennine Way
The Pennine Way Map Booklet
Walking the Dales Way
Walking the Dales Way Map Booklet

NORTH EAST ENGLAND, YORKSHIRE DALES AND PENNINES

Cycling in the Yorkshire Dales
Great Mountain Days in the Pennines
Mountain Biking in the Yorkshire Dales
St Oswald's Way and St Cuthbert's Way
The Cleveland Way and the Yorkshire Wolds Way
The Cleveland Way Map Booklet
The North York Moors

The Reivers Way
The Teesdale Way
Trail and Fell Running in the Yorkshire Dales
Walking in County Durham
Walking in Northumberland
Walking in the North Pennines
Walking in the Yorkshire Dales: North and East
Walking in the Yorkshire Dales: South and West

NORTH WEST ENGLAND AND THE ISLE OF MAN

Cycling the Pennine Bridleway
Isle of Man Coastal Path
The Lancashire Cycleway
The Lune Valley and Howgills
Walking in Cumbria's Eden Valley
Walking in Lancashire
Walking in the Forest of Bowland and Pendle
Walking on the Isle of Man
Walking on the West Pennine Moors
Walks in Silverdale and Arnside

LAKE DISTRICT

Cycling in the Lake District
Great Mountain Days in the Lake District
Joss Naylor's Lakes, Meres and Waters of the Lake District
Lake District Winter Climbs
Lake District: High Level and Fell Walks
Lake District: Low Level and Lake Walks
Mountain Biking in the Lake District
Outdoor Adventures with Children – Lake District
Scrambles in the Lake District – North
Scrambles in the Lake District – South
The Cumbria Way
Trail and Fell Running in the Lake District
Walking the Lake District Fells – Borrowdale
  Buttermere

Coniston
Keswick
Langdale
Mardale and the Far East
Patterdale
Wasdale
Walking the Tour of the Lake District

DERBYSHIRE, PEAK DISTRICT AND MIDLANDS

Cycling in the Peak District
Dark Peak Walks
Scrambles in the Dark Peak
Walking in Derbyshire
Walking in the Peak District – White Peak East
Walking in the Peak District – White Peak West

SOUTHERN ENGLAND

20 Classic Sportive Rides in South East England
20 Classic Sportive Rides in South West England
Cycling in the Cotswolds
Mountain Biking on the North Downs
Mountain Biking on the South Downs
North Downs Way Map Booklet
Walking the South West Coast Path
South West Coast Path Map Booklets
  Vol 1: Minehead to St Ives
  Vol 2: St Ives to Plymouth
  Vol 3: Plymouth to Poole
Suffolk Coast and Heath Walks
The Cotswold Way
The Cotswold Way Map Booklet
The Great Stones Way
The Kennet and Avon Canal
The Lea Valley Walk
The North Downs Way
The Peddars Way and Norfolk Coast Path
The Pilgrims' Way
The Ridgeway National Trail
The Ridgeway Map Booklet
The South Downs Way

The South Downs Way Map Booklet
The Thames Path
The Thames Path Map Booklet
The Two Moors Way
The Two Moors Way Map Booklet
Walking Hampshire's Test Way
Walking in Cornwall
Walking in Essex
Walking in Kent
Walking in London
Walking in Norfolk
Walking in the Chilterns
Walking in the Cotswolds
Walking in the Isles of Scilly
Walking in the New Forest
Walking in the North Wessex Downs
Walking on Dartmoor
Walking on Guernsey
Walking on Jersey
Walking on the Isle of Wight
Walking the Jurassic Coast
Walks in the South Downs National Park

WALES AND WELSH BORDERS

Cycle Touring in Wales
Cycling Lon Las Cymru
Glyndwr's Way
Great Mountain Days in Snowdonia
Hillwalking in Shropshire
Hillwalking in Wales – Vols 1&2
Mountain Walking in Snowdonia
Offa's Dyke Path
Offa's Dyke Map Booklet
Ridges of Snowdonia
Scrambles in Snowdonia
Snowdonia: 30 Low-level and easy walks – North
Snowdonia: 30 Low-level and easy walks – South
The Cambrian Way
The Ceredigion and Snowdonia Coast Paths
The Pembrokeshire Coast Path
The Pembrokeshire Coast Path Map Booklet

The Severn Way
The Snowdonia Way
The Wales Coast Path
The Wye Valley Walk
Walking in Carmarthenshire
Walking in Pembrokeshire
Walking in the Forest of Dean
Walking in the Wye Valley
Walking on Gower
Walking on the Brecon Beacons
Walking the Shropshire Way

MOUNTAIN LITERATURE

8000 metres
A Walk in the Clouds
Abode of the Gods
Fifty Years of Adventure
The Pennine Way – the Path, the People, the Journey
Unjustifiable Risk?

TECHNIQUES

Fastpacking
Geocaching in the UK
Map and Compass
Outdoor Photography
Polar Exploration
The Mountain Hut Book

MINI GUIDES

Alpine Flowers
Navigation
Pocket First Aid and Wilderness Medicine
Snow

For full information on all our guides, books and eBooks, visit our website:
www.cicerone.co.uk